IF MY PEOPLE PRAY

An Eleventh-Hour Call to Prayer and Revival

D0019302

Randy Maxwell

IF MY PEOPLE PRAY

An Eleventh-Hour Call to Prayer and Revival

Randy Maxwell

Pacific Press Publishing Association
Boise, Idaho
Oshawa, Ontario, Canada

Edited by Bonnie Tyson-Flyn
Designed by Dennis Ferree
Calligraphy by Timothy Botts
Typeset in 13/16 Adobe Garamond

Unless otherwise noted, all Scripture quotations are taken from the New International Version.

The author assumes full responsibility for the accuracy of all facts and quotations cited in this book.

Library of Congress Cataloging-in-Publication Data:
Maxwell, Randy.
     If my people pray : an eleventh-hour call to prayer and revival /
Randy Maxwell.
          p.   cm.
     ISBN 0-8163-1246-X.
     1. Seventh-day Adventists—Membership. 2. Bible. O. T.
Chronicles, 2nd, VII, 14—Devotional literature. 3. Prayer—
Christianity. 4. Revivals. 5. Church renewal—Seventh-day
Adventists.   I. Title.
     BX6154.M36   1995
     243—dc20   94-37661
                                                              CIP

95 96 97 98 99 • 5 4 3 2 1

Contents

Dedication

To
my three daughters:
Candice Denae, Crystal Marie, and
Danielle Simone.

Love the Lord your God,
listen to his voice,
and hold fast to him.
For the Lord is your life.
(Deuteronomy 30:20)

CHAPTER 1

It's Time to Pray!

"The hour has come for you to wake up from your slumber,
because our salvation is nearer now than
when we first believed"
(Romans 13:11).

I don't often make claims of hearing God speak. But this time His voice was clear and insistent.

I sat at one of several long tables arranged in a hollow square in our church's fellowship hall. The occasion was a church board meeting. The discussion was the future of the church in light of its failure to reach the Baby Boomers and the disastrous implications of doing the same with their offspring, the Busters.

There was talk of studies being done, of surveys being taken, of various church models that needed scrutiny, and of books and seminars written to address the problem. At one point, a frustrated and genuinely puzzled individual from the World War II generation asked no one in particular, "What exactly was it that the church failed to do for the Baby Boomers?"

A young man not much older than I decided the time had come to clear the air on this painful subject and proceeded to respond with an eloquence and pathos that held the room spellbound.

The furrowed brow of the older man conveyed equal parts of concern, pain, and confusion. He was trying to understand what this young man, who had once been a hair's breadth away from leaving the church, but was now a dedicated conference worker, was saying. But he wasn't getting it. And again he asked the younger man to show specifically where the church had dropped the ball.

It was during this exchange that I heard Him.

"Until My people come together in prayer and repent of the hurt they've done to Me and to each other, none of this other stuff will ever make a difference." My pulse quickened with the intensity of the message. "You can have all the seminars and books and studies and committees and strategies and plans you want, but until you seek Me first with all your hearts, it is all in vain."

My chest hurt from my heart's frantic pounding. I felt as if a dam within me was on the verge of bursting. It was all I could do to keep from blurting out, "Stop! God wants us to pray!" Maybe I should have done it. I didn't then, but I'm saying it now.

It's time to pray!

Why? Because slowly, sleepily, and almost imperceptibly, we're losing the ability to believe in a risen Saviour who gets His hands dirty in the sweat and grime of our lives. A God who is real and active and makes a difference! Jesus left the tomb two thousand years ago, but we've managed to bury Him under a pile of religious trivia and petty infighting that keeps Him distant and removed from anything meaningful to our lives.

We're going through all the right motions, doing all the right things, saying all the right phrases. But the truth is, we're dying of thirst for contact with the living God! And though many of us continue to drag ourselves to church, week in and week out, the desert that has formed beneath our well-rehearsed, supple exteriors continues to grow. We look good on the surface, but underneath we're parched and shriveled.

It's like the yeast infection we've been trying to get rid of in our youngest daughter Danielle. After weeks of antibiotics to stop recurrent ear and sinus infections, Dani came down with the mother of all diaper rashes. When her diaper was full, she would whimper, pull on it to get it away from her skin, and walk as if she'd been riding a horse.

Being good parents and not wanting our child to suffer, we whipped out the Desitin and waited for the rash to clear up. It didn't. In fact, it started to look as if her skin had been burned.

We took her to see her pediatrician, and he promptly diagnosed the "diaper rash" as a yeast infection. We were given a prescription for a medicinal cream called Tridesilon, which was to be applied three times a day.

It wasn't long before we started noticing a real improvement in Dani's rash. The "burn" area grew lighter, and the angry red bumps began to disappear. Then, just when we thought we were getting the upper hand on the infection, the bumps made a vicious comeback. Dani began pulling at her diaper again, and her skin started to look like it did before we started applying the Tridesilon.

Back to the doctor we went, and it was this second trip that revealed the source of our daughter's problem. The cream we had been given was only a topical treatment. Tridesilon could clear up the bumps on the surface, but it contained no medicine to kill the yeast underneath.

Why we weren't told this from the beginning, I don't know, but all we had really done was prolong our baby's suffering. We had been treating the symptom without dealing with the cause. And for many of us, our religion has taken the form of a topical treatment that smooths the bumps on the surface but can't scratch the burning itch of our infected souls.

I want to be straight with you and straight with myself. I've talked with many people who feel that our worship services have become a nuisance—a wearying round of formality that has no more relevance to the problems they wrestle with during the week than does a slide rule on today's information superhighway.

The effects of our spiritual thirst are unmistakable and painful. The hard hearts. The sharp tongues. The long, pinched faces of those who claim to be redeemed. The congregations that continue long histories of devouring pastors and squelching change of any kind. The absence of our young people. An unhealthy isolation that cuts us off from the people we're supposed to be saving and a love for "truth" above a love for people that saps our ability to be compassionate and makes us "as barren of the Spirit of God as were the hills of Gilboa of dew and rain."[1] These are symptoms of a condition that only Jesus can cure.

It's time to pray!

Please don't tune me out. I know you pray. It's the one Christian practice we are taught almost from the cradle. Before we can read, we know how to pray.

But prayer can be seen as so much religious busywork. And to some, it seems a cop-out from rolling up our sleeves and doing the "real work" of Christianity. The promise "I'm praying for you" is perceived by many Christians to be a mask that projects piety but hides a lazy, indifferent attitude on the part of the pray-er.

But this is not the kind of prayer I'm talking about. This is a book about revival praying. The kind of praying that we as a people must enter into and practice in order to see real and lasting change in our church and in our lives. It's about honesty and coming to terms with where we really are spiritually and admitting how much we need Jesus.

This book is *not* about how to get God to do what you want. Or how to create a heavenly Burger King where you can have the blessings "your way, right away." If this is what you're looking for, you've dialed the wrong number.

But if you, like me, are anxious to experience the kind of communion with God that will break you free from bland, powerless, status-quo Christianity and put you where the action is—face to face and heart to heart with *Jehovah-ropheka* (the God who heals), then let's talk. Or better still, let's *pray!* Nothing else we can do or say or debate or theorize can bring about the revival of true godliness we so desperately need as can prayer. And I believe God is calling His church to prayer as never before.

I want to invite you to explore with me one of the greatest promises and calls to prayer in the Bible. Second Chronicles 7:14 has been set to music, interjected in countless speeches and sermons, and has become almost as familiar to Christians as the twenty-third Psalm. But our familiarity with the text can cause us to overlook the power of what is being said.

"If my people, who are called by my name, will humble themselves and pray and seek my face and turn from their wicked ways, then will I hear from heaven and will forgive their sin and will heal their land."

I believe that right here in the forty words of this promise, God is outlining the method by which members of a lukewarm church may purchase "gold refined in the fire, so [we] can become rich; and white clothes to wear, so [we] can cover [our] shameful nakedness; and salve to put on [our] eyes, so [we] can see" (Revelation 3:18). Here is described the currency we must use to "buy" from Jesus the antidote for our spiritual sickness. Do you see the similarities in the prescriptions? *"If anyone hears My voice and opens the door, I will come!"* *"If*

My people will humble themselves and pray, I will hear, forgive, and heal!"

The door to a new relationship with Christ is opened by prayer. It is a relationship we cannot live without—and an offer we can hardly afford to refuse. Throughout this book, I'm going to look at this incredible promise phrase by phrase. The words of the text itself will form the basic structure and determine the progression of my thoughts. By doing this, I believe we will hear, maybe as never before, the plea of our Father's heart for His children to turn to Him for the healing that only He can provide.

And maybe, just maybe, before we commission another survey or hire another consultant or attend another seminar, we will try it God's way and discover that He is "able to do immeasurably more than all we ask or imagine" (Ephesians 3:20).

It's time to pray!

Right now, as you read these words, don't you long to touch Him? To hear His voice? Doesn't your spirit cry out for the living water He promises will flow in us like an eternal fountain? Then join me in this prayer:

Lord, I'm tired of playing this game I call church—of pretending to believe while being eaten up with doubt. I'm weary of pious words, proof texts, petty theological debates, and the form of godliness without the power. I want the real thing, Lord. I want You. I dare to make the same request Moses made when He asked You to show him Your glory. I must see You for who You really are. Why should I settle for shadows when You've promised to share Your very being with me?

Thank You for calling me to prayer. I confess I don't know how to pray, how to really touch Your heart and enter into the joy of Your fellowship, but I want to. As You did to Peter that night on the lake, beckon me to come to You, and I will. Only teach me to keep my eyes on You as I take the first halting, trembling steps.

It's Time to Pray

I must lay hold of You, Lord. And if I am to live or ever hope to know the abundant life You came to give me, You must lay hold of me. Here I am. I come with all my liabilities and fears, but I come. And as I come, Lord, please make my life a miracle of Your love and grace. Amen.

---

1. Ellen G. White, *Testimonies for the Church* (Boise, Idaho: Pacific Press Publishing Association, 1948), 5:166.

Part 1

If

"With God nothing shall be impossible."
—Luke 1:37

"You can do more than pray,
after you have prayed, but you can never do more than pray
until you have prayed."
—A. J. Gordon

**Real prayer won't happen unless
and until you pray.**

If

CHAPTER
2

Imagine

Imagine with me for a moment how life and history would have been different *if*. . .

   . . . President Kennedy had canceled his trip to Dallas or had ridden in a hard-topped car,

   . . . Germany had won World War II,

   . . . NASA had canceled *Challenger*'s launch that frigid January morning in 1986,

   . . . Nixon had destroyed the tapes,

   . . . Israel had retaliated against Iraq during the Gulf War,

   . . . Rodney King had never been beaten,

   . . . the ATF hadn't raided the Branch Davidians' Mt. Carmel compound,

   . . . Martin Luther King, Jr., or Bobby Kennedy had survived,

   . . . Adam hadn't eaten the forbidden fruit,

   . . . Jesus had changed His mind in Gethsemane and gone home to His Father.

Imagine with me, now, how the present and future of the church could be different *if. . .*

"*. . . my people, who are called by my name, will humble themselves and pray and seek my face and turn from their wicked ways, then will I hear from heaven and will forgive their sin and will heal their land.*"

I recently confronted a group of people with this challenge at the conclusion of a thirty-day season of prayer. Then, as now, I focused attention on the tiny two-letter proviso at the beginning of this well-known, but seldom-lived promise—*IF*. Even now, as I write this chapter, I'm moved by the staggering implications of this little word.

IF. IF speaks of potential, of possibilities, of chance. The future could look like this, or it could look like that. The outcome could be this, or it could be that. It all depends on actions that are determined by choices that were once thoughts weighed in the scales of imagined outcomes. And at the center of these thoughts was an *IF* hanging in the balance.

IF. What a powerful word! Its power is greatest when applied to the here and now, where the consequences of our choices still lie in our hands. When the future stretches out before us like two branches of a road. When the choice is still ours to make.

When the *IF* is past, however, its power is usually restricted to the imagination. Here, we can only play mental games with an outcome that could have been *IF only . . .*

I'm sure as you read this, your mind is racing with situations in your own life in which circumstances could have been completely different *if* you had made another choice. I'm thinking of some right now.

If my friend hadn't decided to come home from her European vacation a day early, she wouldn't have booked a flight on Pan Am 103 and perished over Lockerbie, Scotland, when the terrorists' bomb blew it from the sky.

If doctors had opted to follow up my mother-in-law's radical mastectomy with chemotherapy and radiation, perhaps she wouldn't have had a recurrence and died fourteen years later.

If I had taken a job on the East Coast in the summer of 1986, I wouldn't have been available to accept the offer that came from my present employer eight months later in March of 1987.

Destinies hinge, empires crumble, companies succeed, great discoveries are made, careers are launched, morgues are filled, happiness is obtained—because of choices and their consequences. A course of action is pursued, and a result follows. Cause and effect.

What course of action is God asking His people to pursue in 2 Chronicles 7:14? Very simply, He's asking us to humble ourselves, pray, seek His face, and repent. What is the promised result? Heard prayers, forgiven sins, and healing. The promise is fantastic. It's what we need. But it all hangs on the big *IF* at the beginning.

The beginning

Three friends sat at a small, round table one frosty winter morning. The tabletop was strewn with potted plants; squares of paper with inspirational quotes, prayer requests, and scriptures handwritten on them; highlighter pens; Bibles; and small hills of books sporting titles like *The Taste of New Wine*, by Keith Miller; *Waiting on God*, by Andrew Murray; and *Answers to Prayer*, by George Mueller.

This little breakfast nook was the gathering place for my friends and me every Wednesday morning at 6:30 a.m. Here, we met to catch up on each others' lives, encourage each another, share a scripture that was making an impression on us at the moment, pray, and discuss our favorite topic—revival in the church.

It was at one of these Wednesday-morning get-togethers that God challenged me to put my faith where my mouth was. I had waxed very eloquent this particular morning about the possibilities of what God could do if we would pray. It was a great discussion. As men typically do, we philosophized and theorized—sometimes with great passion and sincerity. But it seldom got much farther. Now, however, God was challenging me to put theory to the test. To not just talk about prayer, but to *pray*.

I covenanted with God to meet Him at 4:30 a.m. every Tuesday morning specifically to pray for revival in our church and for our pastor to receive a new vision of ministry. I asked one and then the other of my friends to join me in this covenant.

Our faith was strong and our commitment real, but as time went on, instead of a sense of release, I felt a heaviness and an urgency I couldn't describe. It was like a rock in my chest. A vice that squeezed my throat. I had that strained, lump-in-the-throat feeling you get when you're trying to fight back tears. But I didn't have a clue about what was bugging me.

I talked with my wife, my mom, some trusted friends. I prayed and asked God to tell me clearly what this feeling meant and what He was asking me to do.

Like the buzzer on an alarm clock that starts as a distant, muffled whine in the last foggy remnants of sleep but shrieks with unmistakable clarity once we're fully awake, the "buzzing" within me was suddenly clear. I knew God was calling and what He wanted. He was calling me—and others—to prayer. Purposeful, specific, promise-claiming, revival-seeking, self-renunciative prayer.

I talked it over with my wife, Suzette, and asked if we could have a small gathering in our home. I envisioned six to ten people in our living room, no more. Suzette wasn't so sure. She wondered if our home was the best place for the meeting. Where would the kids go? Was there enough room?

A logical place would have been the church. But I felt it was important that the meeting be perceived as a "grass roots" happening rather than as an official church program. I don't know why I felt this was important, but I did.

Still unsure about the meeting place, we set out a fleece and on

November 6, 1993, put this announcement, minus the locale, in the bulletin:

"What would happen if we humbled ourselves before God and spent some concentrated time in prayer, seeking God's face for vision, revival, and an outpouring of the Holy Spirit?"

I had no idea who would respond, what form our prayer would take, or what to expect. All I knew was that God was asking me to take action—to extend the invitation, to provide the opportunity for His people to pray.

The blurb went on to ask those interested in coming to call Suzette or me at home. And it wasn't long before we received confirmation that God was in the plan.

After the 8:15 a.m. service that next Sabbath, a friend approached me in the hallway and stated her interest in what we were doing. She then offered her home to us for the meeting. I was grateful for her offer but still not convinced a bigger location was necessary.

During the next few days, Suzette began receiving calls from people stating their intentions to come. It soon became apparent that we would need the larger space. I phoned the friend who had made the offer of her home and asked if her invitation still stood. After she graciously confirmed, I changed the announcement for the next Sabbath's bulletin, giving a specific location for our meeting. The day we were to begin, I was tense with anticipation. I wanted to arrive early and take a few minutes to get myself together before people started arriving. My heart, which was already working hard enough to support the legs and lungs of a long-distance runner, began to throb like a jackhammer when I entered the friend's living room and saw a handful of people with eager, expectant faces, already seated and rarin' to go.

With each ring of the doorbell, my excitement mounted. *Lord! What does this mean?* I asked myself, as it soon became obvious that sofa and chair space was about to disappear. Our host and hostess scrambled to produce extra chairs while the doorbell kept ringing and the people kept coming. By the time we bowed our heads to ask the Lord's blessing on our meeting, thirty-seven people had jammed together, for one purpose—to seek God in prayer.

This represented approximately 11 percent of our total (not just our "active") church membership! I was overwhelmed both at the level of interest and also at the mix of people present. The World War II generation was there. My group—the Baby Boomers—were there. We had couples, singles, our pastor, surgeons, and retired farmers. And they were there because they felt the need to *pray!*

Our purpose and objectives were clear. I handed everyone a sheet of paper with the following statement of mission:

"To provide an opportunity for all who feel the need to engage in a special season of prayer which will last thirty days. During this time we will pray specifically for (1) an outpouring of the Holy Spirit, (2) personal and corporate revival, and (3) God's leading in the discovery of our church's mission and ministry." We were going to covenant to pray daily for these three specific requests.

The last twenty minutes of our hour together was reserved for prayer. We formed the best circle we could in that overcrowded den and got down to the business we were there to perform. As we began to pray, I knew Jesus was right there with us, agreeing with our requests. I felt exhilarated and fulfilled, knowing that we were responding to the Saviour's call and doing what He asked us to do.

The Lord was birthing something new, something fresh and powerful. We were setting aside personal and group agendas and uniting around a single desire to see God glorified in our midst by means of a revived church with a clear mission. The prayers flowed from the lips of the petitioners like music from an orchestra, with the Holy Spirit conducting. There were fervency, determination, entreaty, and a sincerity that are often missing from typical corporate prayer experiences.

We met for five weeks instead of four, moving to the church fellowship hall in order to more comfortably accommodate everyone. Though I kept anticipating a drop in attendance (a lack of faith on my part!), the group never dropped below twenty-four and got as large as thirty-nine.

We prayed for each other, for our children, for our pastor, for unity, for forgiveness, for power to believe the promises in God's Word, for revival, and for hearts set on seeking His face. We prayed in the classrooms, in the foyer, in the pastor's study, and in the sanctuary, asking God to bless those who ministered and worshiped there. And when we reached the last session, we lighted candles and pledged to keep praying—to be lights in the darkness. To keep on keeping on.

But before we lighted those candles on that last evening, we faced again God's big *IF* in 2 Chronicles 7:14. And the same question I asked of our prayer group that fall night I ask again of myself, and I ask of you now. What will we do? How will history and future generations (if time should last) judge us in light of this call to prayer and repentance?

CHAPTER

3

Our Greatest Need

We can't overlook the fact that the *IF* in this text allows the possibility that we *won't* pray. We can choose not to humble ourselves, not to seek His face, not to turn from our wicked ways.

Maybe we don't need God to hear from heaven. Perhaps we don't need our sins forgiven or our land healed. After all, we no longer live in an agrarian society where our livelihood depends on rain. The locusts of verse 13 can't eat bank cards, safe-deposit boxes, or new Jeep Cherokees with antilock brakes and a driver's-side airbag.

So why pay attention to this warning and this promise? It doesn't seem to apply. What is the very worst that could happen if we didn't heed this advice? Frankly, the very worst thing that could happen is that we stay *exactly* as we are. And exactly how are we? "Wretched, pitiful, poor, blind and naked" (Revelation 3:17). This assessment comes from the True Witness, not from me.

Make no mistake. I love this church. There are a lot of good, positive, praiseworthy things to say about it. But we must also be honest and admit that despite the good, we are hurting big time. And for many, the pain runs deep.

Because we no longer take time to study God's Word for ourselves, many are "infants, tossed back and forth by the waves, and blown here and there by every wind of teaching and by the cunning and craftiness of men in their deceitful scheming" (Ephesians 4:14). Many of our members are fodder for self-appointed, would-be champions of "new light," who undermine trust in the organized work and cause the people to view anything from the General Conference or its institutions with suspicion. Our baptistries are filled with cobwebs; our attempts at outreach are weak and ineffective. Our young people are absent from our worship services, and, if we were brutally honest, we'll admit that, like them, we're bored stiff.

I recently attended a Christmas program at a sister church during the holiday season. The decorations were festive, the singing was superb, the musicians were excellent. Everything was as it should be—except for one thing. There was no joy! When the congregation joined the choir in a medley of Christmas carols, there was no life in the singing. No evidence that the living Christ was among us, no celebrating His entrance as a tiny baby into our hopeless existence.

That service was in stark contrast to a five-year-old videotaped Christmas program that never fails to move me to tears whenever I view it. The joy of the season and the awe and wonder that is Christmas comes through every number—whether by choir, orchestra, or congregation. I wish I could say that this was a tape of an Adventist program, but I cannot.

Where is our joy?

Too often, our services seem to portray a "god of the past, who fits neatly into the box of our predetermined patterns and, to the great relief of many, never does anything remotely unexpected, never causes his servants to move beyond the bounds of what is humanly explainable, and never does anything supernatural."[1]

It's as I once heard Wintley Phipps say in a sermon, "In our churches we have the coronation without the presence of the king. We have high processionals and dignified recessionals. And when the people leave, they whisper to one another: 'That was nice, but where was the King?' "

Where, indeed!

A. W. Tozer has said, "It is a solemn thing, and no small scandal in the Kingdom, to see God's children starving while actually seated at the Father's table."[2] How many men—upstanding, hard-working, committed Christians—have told me that the only reason they attend church is because of their kids. They want their children to have a solid spiritual foundation, but as for them, they get precious little out of the corporate worship experience.

Look around you. Where are the thirty- to forty-five-year-olds? Why have they stopped coming? What are their needs? Do we even care? Where do the young couples with children go after Sabbath School? Do more Adventists than non-Adventists show up for your evangelistic meetings? Does your church even conduct evangelistic meetings?

Every year at Pacific Press, where I work, we view the General Conference president's "State of the Church" address on video. I watched this year's address and noted with pride the reports that came from the world field about baptisms, new churches being built, and previously unreached countries being entered. When the report turned to North America, however, the news focused on disaster relief and community services. This was great news and certainly cause for rejoicing, but painfully obvious by its absence was news concerning church growth and evangelism.

What are we doing? Where is the power?

I occasionally sit in on a personal-issues Bible-study class at our church that is under the direction of my close friend and prayer partner. I like this class because of the honesty that comes from the people who attend. Some are long-time Adventists who've drifted and are taking their first tentative steps back. They've been burned, and they're having to unlearn a lot of guilt-inducing junk that's distorted their view of God.

Recently, the discussion focused on the fruit of the Spirit, and we eventually got around to talking about joy and peace—and the lack of these blessings in many of their lives. When class was over, I pulled my friend aside and said, "You know, let's just say that the church failed to reach the world for God. Admit that we blew it. We were irrelevant. We failed to make a difference outside our doors."

I'm sure he wondered where I was going with this. I continued: "But if we could say that at least we did make a difference to and among our own, we could claim some victory. We could say that it worked for us—that our religion made a difference in our own lives." I lowered my voice then. "But as selfish as that statement would be, we can't even say that. It's not even working for us!"

Our religion is failing to make a difference even among our own. Increasingly, we're just as miserable, confused, and without the peace and joy and hope of Christ as the "lost" outside our church doors. We're like the coin in Jesus' parable (see Luke 15)—we're lost *inside* the house!

And we're back where we started in 2 Chronicles 7:14. What will we do?

Our time is now

I have a section of a 1988 newspaper commemorating the twentieth anniversary of Senator Robert F. Kennedy's assassination. One of the stories in this section is entitled "Hope died on hotel kitchen floor." In the article, California assemblyman Tom Hayden is quoted as saying: "Part of me feels the emptiness of missed possibilities and always will. . . . There will never be another Robert Kennedy. . . . There will never be a time as poignant or important, but there is work to be done."[3]

What about us today? Is our time now? Will the hopes of a revived church die on the living-room floors of Christians who can't find time to kneel there and ask God for what we need most? Will the hopes of Boomer- and Buster-generation members die on the board-room floors of churches and conferences, where discouraged leaders throw up their hands more often than they fall to their knees? Will ours be an era of missed possibilities? Will we continue on as we are? Will we continue to argue, point fingers, do studies, draft new proposals, form more committees, launch more programs, attend more seminars? Or will we do what God asks? "The church's greatest deficiency today is in power," says Alvin J. Vander Griend. "Not in programs, strategies, materials, or ideas. And power for ministry can be released only through prayer."[4]

James Kilpatrick, a nationally syndicated columnist, wrote about a speech he considers the greatest he ever heard. The speech, entitled "Will the future redeem the past?" was given by Charles Malik, Lebanon's ambassador to the United States in the mid-50s and later president of the U.N. General Assembly. Malik was the principal speaker at a Williamsburg, Virginia, ceremony marking that state's Declaration of Rights of 1776.

That June afternoon in 1960, this philosopher and diplomat spoke of "a life-and-death struggle between international communism and the rest of the world, especially the Western world, and in the Western world especially the United States of America." Malik then painted a picture of what the West could have done to prevent the Communist gains that then claimed a third of humankind.

With passion and eloquence, he launched into the heart of his subject and declared: "If only people rose to the occasion, if only they were not overwhelmed by their softness and apathy, if only they overcame their greed, if only they were morally strong, if only they were not selfish and narrow, if only they were not petty and spiteful and stupid, if only they were big, if only they knew what was at stake, if only they were not hypocritical, if only they trampled underfoot the wide and easy way."[5]

Will the future redeem our past? Malik spoke of a "life-and-death struggle" with Communism. Today, we are engaged in a "life-and-death struggle" against "the rulers, against the authorities, against the powers of this dark world and against the spiritual forces of evil in the heavenly realms" (Ephesians 6:12). What will we do to halt the enemy's gains in and outside God's church? Will we rise to the occasion? Will we shake off our softness and apathy? Can we stop being petty, spiteful, and narrow? Can we realize what's at stake?

All across this nation and around the world, Christians are responding to God's call to prayer. They are meeting in small groups, in churches, and in stadiums. They're taking prayer to the streets of their neighborhoods and along the borders of countries they've claimed for Christ. It's a movement that is causing many learned observers, like Dr. Peter Wagner, the well-known church-growth writer and professor at Fuller Theological Seminary, to say, "I sincerely believe that we are now in the beginning stages of the greatest movement of prayer in living memory."[6]

Is there something here for us to learn? Is our need of revival less than other Christians'? Are we so well-off spiritually that we can ignore this most urgent call?

Writing to the Adventist Church, Ellen White states: "A revival of true godliness among us is the greatest and most urgent of all our needs. To seek this should be our first work."[7] A few sentences later, she provides the method by which this work is to be done. "A revival need be expected only in answer to prayer."[8]

The fork in the road

What would happen *if* we as a people stopped playing church long enough to do the one thing we need to do most—to pray?

What would happen *if* we took God's Word to heart and began to seek His face for genuine and lasting revival?

I believe there is a growing hunger among God's people for a living faith in a living God. There is a restlessness and a desire to dispense with business as usual. Small groups are forming. Women's and men's ministries are being organized, and individuals are establishing prayer partnerships for encouragement and accountability.

Growing numbers of Adventist Christians are weary of the petty infighting, irrelevant squabbles over fine points of theology, and the lack of love displayed in the many power struggles we engage in to preserve our version of the truth. We're tired of the criticism, fault-finding, and parochial attitudes that keep us shut up in our own little world, out of reach and out of touch with the people we're supposed to be loving and winning for Christ.

The good news is that there is an answer to the deep cry of our hearts, and that answer is prayer. In my own life I'm being rejuvenated in my Christian experience by what I'm learning about prayer. The more I pray and the more I read, the more I believe that the most exciting days of the church are just ahead of us.

The power and blessings of heaven await our demand and reception. The day is coming when the mountains of discouragement, spiritual lethargy, tame message, lost purpose, and powerlessness can and will be thrown "into the sea" at our command (see Mark 11:23). But that day will come only *IF* we "humble [ourselves] and pray"!

I must confess to you that I have my fears concerning this book. For months, I didn't want anyone to know I was thinking of writing it because I wasn't sure if the timing was right or if God wanted me to take the assignment. I'm not the classic picture of the "prayer warrior." I see myself as a student in Christ's school of prayer—with *so* much more to learn.

But I've decided to put my faith where my mouth is and follow God wherever He leads. I urge you to join me. We're about to embark upon a rewarding journey. We stand, as it were, at that mythical fork in the road where the future stretches before us, and the choice is still ours to make. You've come this far with me; come a little farther.

What can we expect as we plumb the depths of this magnificent promise of God's provision?

First, *we will discover our fantastic privileges as redeemed children of God.* Many of us have no idea what our Saviour has done for us and wants to do in us. We are "eagles roosting in sparrows' nests." Our discovery of prayer will bring us into contact with our amazing inheritance as God's children—heirs of every spiritual blessing in Christ (see Ephesians 1:3).

Second, *we will come to understand our reason for being here.* Why are we Christians anyway? If our purpose for being here is to love our families; live clean, moral lives; and pay our taxes on time, we could join EST or Amway or the Kiwanis Club. We need to recapture the true purpose of being disciples. God wants to make us the executors of His will and establish His kingdom on earth through us. Understanding this one fact alone will revolutionize our prayer life and bring new vitality to our corporate worship.

Third, *our God will get bigger.* I know that sounds weird, but our God has gotten altogether too small. We box Him in so tightly with our preferences, traditions, cultural Christianity, and religious forms that He can't have control. And, frankly, we like it that way. But when God is made in our image, we can't have much faith in Him. He's too much like us—unreliable, wishy-washy, weak, and preoccupied. Ah, but when we pray in the Spirit—with spiritual insight and according to His will—God grows to enormous proportions. He becomes our all in all—the source of our joy, the reason and focus for our worship, the author and finisher of our faith—and His glory fills not only our lives, but the whole earth! Don't you long to worship a God who is alive? Who is in control? Who makes a difference in your life and those around you today? You will meet this God in prayer.

Fourth, *we will hear and recognize God's call to repentance.* It's not a popular subject, and I'm not likely to win many friends on this subject. Nevertheless, true healing cannot occur unless and until we face the source of our illness and "turn from our wicked ways." We must stop blaming everyone and everything around us for the church's ills and ask God to help us see where we are culpable, where we've failed. Repentance, like grace, is a gift. And, like grace, it will set us free if we let it.

Finally, *we will find the love of our lives—Jesus.* To know Him. To love Him. To embrace Him. To walk with Him. To be assured of His living presence, His acceptance, His forgiveness. To know His will and to be called into partnership with Him in the execution of that will—this will be our life, our joy, our all.

He has promised to be found by us *IF* we seek Him with all our hearts (see Jeremiah 29:13, 14). What will you do?

No turning back

I have one of those calendars that has an inspirational thought for each day of the year. Oliver Wendell Holmes was responsible for the thought on January 10, which read: "Man's mind, once stretched by a new idea, never again regains its original dimensions."

My mind, heart, and soul are being stretched by the "new" idea that prayer really does change things—that God is about do something "marvelous in our eyes." I've had a chance to see just a little of what is possible with the tiniest seed of faith in a God who fills the universe—a God who calls me "son" and invites me to share His throne.

I can't go back. I don't want to. Will you join me in seeking Him will all your heart? I urge you to say Yes to God's call to prayer. Yes to His promise of healing. Yes to His invitation to experience "immeasurably more than all we ask or imagine" (Ephesians 3:20).

As we journey, let's travel with this prayer that I have pasted on the inside cover of my Bible:

"O God, I have tasted Thy goodness, and it has both satisfied me and made me thirsty for more. I am painfully conscious of my need of further grace. I am ashamed of my lack of desire. O God, the Triune God, I want to want Thee; I long to be filled with longing; I thirst to be made more thirsty still. Show me Thy glory, I pray Thee, so that I may know Thee indeed. Begin in mercy a new work of love within me. Say to my soul, 'Rise up, my love, my fair one, and come away.' Then give me grace to rise and follow Thee up from this misty lowland where I have wandered so long. In Jesus' name. Amen." [9]

---

1. Graham Kendrick, *Learning to Worship as a Way of Life* (Minneapolis: Bethany House Publishers, 1984), 18.

2. A. W. Tozer, *The Pursuit of God* (Camp Hill, Penn.: Christian Publications, Inc., 1982), 9.

3. *The Idaho Press-Tribune*, 5 June 1988, C-1.

4. Alvin J. Vander Griend, *The Praying Church Sourcebook* (Grand Rapids, Mich.: Church Development Resources, 1990), 4.

5. James Kilpatrick, "Greatest Speech I Have Ever Heard," *The Idaho Press Tribune*, 20 January 1988,

6. *The Praying Church Sourcebook*, 3.

7. Ellen G. White, *Selected Messages* (Washington, D.C.: Review and Herald Publishing Association, 1958), 1:121.

8. Ibid.

9. *The Pursuit of God*, 20.

Part 2

My people

"Fear not, for I have redeemed you;
I have summoned you by name; you are mine."
—Isaiah 43:1

"The knowledge of God's Father-love is the first and simplest,
but also the last and highest lesson in the school of prayer."
—Andrew Murray

Real prayer happens when you go to your knees
knowing that the God you're talking to wants you.
That you belong to each other.

CHAPTER
4

The Power of Belonging

I'm holding one of our many photo albums in my lap and looking into faces of those I love. On one page my cousin Pam stands next to her handsome son Todd. I remember when he was born, his many near-death bouts with asthma, his love of airplanes and flying. Now I look at him standing next to his mom, almost a head taller than she. Time flies.

Across the page, my Aunt Gloria holds her newest grandson. Her face is stretched into that characteristic proud smile of a grandma. "Dean," as we call her, couldn't be any other way. She thinks all the kids in the family (not just hers, but *all* of us—nephews, nieces, and all our children) walk on water. In her eyes we can do no wrong. She's our Pollyanna, and we tease her unmercifully. But it's great to know that someone is always in your corner, cheering you on.

I flip a few pages, and there's my wife's mother. I remember now how pretty she was. She sits with legs crossed in her living-room chair, wearing a smart green suit with a delicate white blouse. I check the date on the back of the photo and see that it was taken in November 1989. Two years after her cancer had recurred.

She's asleep in Jesus now. We miss her terribly. My five-year-old still prays for her grandma. We've talked to her about it, tried to explain things. But we don't scold her. Her love won't let her stop praying for Grandma.

In this photo, however, there's no hint of disease. Only grace, beauty, and that cherubic smile that we are still blessed to see in the face of our youngest daughter, Danielle.

Each page in this album brings me face to face with people I love. With images that produce a memory, a smile, and a smorgasbord of emotions. These are "my people." People with whom I share blood, laughter, tears, a heritage, a history. My history. We're family. And family means something.

At its best, family means continuity, nurture, caring, support, love, identity, and belonging. At its worst, it can mean hurt, distrust, estrangement, rejection, and abuse. A lot depends on who your people are, whom you belong to.

Psalm 23 introduces us to someone who is proud of whom he belongs to. Putting himself into the role of a sheep, David says proudly, "The Lord is *my* shepherd; I shall not want" (Psalm 23:1, KJV, emphasis mine). You can almost see this sheep puff out his chest with pride as he addresses others less fortunate than he. "I belong to the Lord. He is *my* owner and provider. Because of this, I will lack nothing."

Is there a feeling more wonderful than that of belonging? Of knowing that you are accepted, loved, and valued just for being you? I have no data to back me up, but I believe that the growth of gangs in this country is directly related to a young person's need to belong.

I remember an urgent phone call I received a few years ago from a local school principal. He spoke slowly and with concern for a young girl we both knew who had run away from home. Apparently, she was very depressed—even suicidal. The principal had done what he could to encourage her and connect her with the pastor, but he was afraid she might hurt herself and asked me to call her at the number she'd given him.

I nervously muttered a prayer for wisdom as I dialed the number and waited for her to come on the line.

Between sobs and periods of tense silence, I was able to piece together a tale of anger, loneliness, and rejection. She felt as if nothing she did was good enough for her mother and that she didn't feel welcome in her own home. The more she talked, the more she confided in me, and before long, she admitted that she had joined a gang. I pressed her for an explanation. With sounds of rock music and laughter in the background, she replied, "Because these guys are my family. They give me a place to belong."

A place to belong

A place to belong! A circle of people who make us feel special, needed, and desired. Isn't this the cry of every heart? The secret wish of the runaway, the gang banger, the prostitute, the honor student, the homemaker, and the preacher?

In his book *Habitation of Dragons*, Keith Miller tells a moving story of a small-group encounter with a middle-aged woman who opened a window onto her painful past as an orphan.

We were in a small group of adults who were struggling together to learn how to pray and to live as Christians. We were getting acquainted by going around the room, each telling the others some things about his childhood. One older lady had had a good many disappointments and seemed bitter about her past. Then it was Alice's turn. She spoke to us hesitantly.

"When I was a tiny little girl, I was put in an orphanage. I was not pretty at all, and no one wanted me. But I can recall longing to be adopted and loved by a family as far back as I can remember. I thought about it day and night. But everything I did seemed to go wrong. I tried too hard to please everybody who came to look me over, and all I did was drive people away. Then one day the head of the orphanage told me a family was going to come and take me home with them. I was so excited, I jumped up and down and cried. The matron reminded me that I was on trial and that it might not be a permanent arrangement. But I just knew it would be. So I went with this family and started to school in their town—a very happy little girl. And life began to open for me, just a little.

"But one day, a few months later, I skipped home from school and ran in the front door of the big old house we lived in. No one was at home, but there in the middle of the front hall was my battered old suitcase with my little coat thrown over it. As I stood there and looked at that suitcase, it slowly dawned on me what it meant . . . they didn't want me. And I hadn't even suspected." '

What a pathetic statement! *They didn't want me!* She had no one to call her own, no one to belong to. Yet, whether we have parents or not, whether estranged from our families or loved unconditionally by them, God calls us *His* people. "The sheep of *his* pasture" (Psalm 100:3, emphasis mine).

We belong. All the time. In summer, in fall. In winter, in spring. In bed, on the job. At the market, on our knees. Under stress, overdrawn. Bad hair day, good hair day. In traffic, all alone. Changing a tire, changing a diaper. At the computer, at the cleaners. On the golf course, taking a college course. On cloud nine or in tunnel 57. It doesn't matter. Wherever we are, however we feel, whatever we're doing, *God wants us!* We belong. We're *His* people.

Do you believe that? No, I'm not asking if you understand what

I'm saying. I'm bypassing your head for a moment and aiming for your heart. Do you really believe that God *wants* you? That you are His treasured possession and that no one else—no matter how witty, good looking, well dressed, talented, charismatic, intelligent, or spiritual—can take your place in His heart?

Our greatest struggle

The longer I'm in this church, the more people I find whose greatest struggle is to believe that God loves them. *Surprise,* all you theory-loving theologians out there! The people in our pews aren't losing sleep over the nature of Christ, the historical-critical method of interpreting Scripture, or which apartment of the heavenly sanctuary Jesus is ministering in. They cry out in the midst of the never-ceasing, never-slowing treadmill of their lives for some assurance that God loves and cares for them.

Just yesterday, I sat in a Sabbath School class where a fortysomething woman who had been raised in this church confessed that the God she knew wasn't a God she could come to for a little TLC. I noticed how still the room had suddenly become as she spoke. After years of dedicated service to the church, this woman was going through one of the toughest desert experiences of her Christian life. Illness, job loss, and a teenager in rebellion were shaking her faith to its very foundation. Her honesty was uncommon in a church setting where the I'm-fine-and-perfect-in-every-way masks are usually three or four deep on everyone.

Clutching a wad of tissue, this woman said that even though her understanding was slowly changing, she still had a hard time coming to God for help, because, in her words, "He's scary." She didn't feel *wanted* by this God—the God she was raised to fear. The God she had been serving all these years was a God who demanded absolute perfection and had no tolerance for failure of any kind. Coming to this God for love and acceptance and understanding was unthinkable.

I'll ask again. Do you really believe that God wants you? That you belong? That you're His? I know it's hard. We can be so unlovable at times. I need reminding. We all do.

At the beginning of his book *The Applause of Heaven,* Max Lucado tells about the rigorous titling process his publishers went through. "In my mind, the scales were tipped in favor of *The Applause of Heaven* when my editor, Carol, read part of the manuscript to some of the Word executives. She read a portion of the book that describes our final journey into the city of God. She read some thoughts I wrote about God's hunger to have his children home, about how he longs to welcome us and may even applaud when we enter the gates.

"After Carol read this section, she noticed one of the men was brushing away a tear. He explained his emotion by saying, 'It's hard for me to imagine God applauding for me.' "[2]

Do you nod your head in agreement with this publishing executive? Then hear the longing in the words of a God who calls us *His people*. A God who does applaud for you. A God who, when approached by Satan with the price for our souls, pointed at His throne, His heaven, and His life and said, "Take it all. Just let My people go."

We're His. We belong. But what's the real significance of this? What does it mean to me today to be one of God's people?

---

1. Keith Miller, *Habitation of Dragons* (Waco, Tex.: Word Books, 1970), 183, 184.

2. Max Lucado, *The Applause of Heaven* (Irving, Tex.: Word Publishing, 1990), xiii.

CHAPTER

5

We're Family

First off, to be God's people means we are family. We're kin.

I recently received a letter on official-looking stationery inviting me and my family to a one-of-a-kind reunion of Maxwells in Ireland. Someone had meticulously tracked down as many American Maxwells as he could for the purpose of bringing together the splintered branches of the Maxwell family tree in the "mother land" of Ireland.

The event described sounded fabulous. Tours of medieval castles where Maxwells once ruled and stops in quaint Irish pubs where we'd "raise a few" with the boys and hear stories about Maxwells from long ago. My wife and I couldn't help but laugh at the prospect of showing up and watching the faces of our long-lost "relatives" as they tried to figure out how these Black people crashed their party. We may share a name, but we have a very different bloodline and history.

When we say Yes to Jesus and accept His invitation to follow Him, whatever our color or language or history, we become "children of God—children born not of natural descent, nor of human decision or a husband's will, but born of God" (John 1:12, 13).

What does it mean for me to be able to call God "Daddy"? To know that I've been invited to "share in the very being of God" (2 Peter 1:4, NEB)? Among other things, it means I do not have to be afraid of Him. I don't have to shake with terror when I approach Him, as the cowardly lion did before the great OZ. He's my Father, and my Father loves me. "For you did not receive a spirit that makes you a slave again to fear, but you received the Spirit of sonship. And by him we cry, 'Abba, Father' " (Romans 8:15).

I know that for some of you, the image of God as Father doesn't help. Your own father may have been abusive, distant, demanding, and impossible to impress or please. Even as an adult, you may still have to battle your nerves whenever you are around him. To you, *father* and *fear* are synonymous.

If this is so, calling God "Father" may not evoke feelings of warmth and love. But what about Jesus? How do you feel about Him? If in Christ you find the compassion, respect, devotion, esteem, and caring you've always longed for, then realize that this same Jesus told Philip, "Anyone who has seen me has seen the Father" (John 14:9).

Jesus wasn't acting alone when He came here to effect our rescue. "God [the Father] was in Christ, reconciling the world unto himself" (2 Corinthians 5:19, KJV). And so that there would be no misunderstanding regarding God's role and heart in our redemption, Jesus said, "In that day you will ask in my name. I am not saying that I will ask the Father on your behalf. No, *the Father himself loves you*" (John 16:26, emphasis mine).

The Bible is replete with stories, prophecies, poems, letters, prayers, and declarations of God's love for us. But for some reason that can be explained only by sin's crippling effect on our minds and hearts, we feel more like orphans than we do sons and daughters of God.

We're Family

And this may be one of the most important reasons for us to respond to God's call to prayer. And perhaps one of God's greatest motivations for extending the invitation. If we come to Him with humility, with repentance, and with our desperate need for acceptance, He promises to "heal our land"—that damaged part of our innermost beings that struggles to embrace God's favor, to believe that we are His treasured possession. His people.

Prayer is how we fight

Our Father wants to give us divine power to "demolish arguments and every pretension that sets itself up against the knowledge of God" (2 Corinthians 10:5). Every lie spun from the pit of hell that contradicts the truth of our standing before God, of our status in His family, is to be blown to smithereens with the weapons God has given us to fight with. And the only offensive weapon God has provided is "the sword of the Spirit, which is the word of God" (Ephesians 6:17). That Word declares, "Fear not, for I have redeemed you; I have summoned you by name; *you are mine!*" (Isaiah 43:1, emphasis mine).

And it is only in prayer that we will receive this divine power. Prayer is not another weapon in our spiritual arsenal. It is *how we fight!* Prayer is the battle plan. It is how we engage the enemy.

Haven't you ever wondered why so many of us are such defeated Christians, when we know all the right doctrines and all the right texts? We've heard all this before. In Sabbath School, at retreats, from pastors, in books and seminars. And yet we can't seem to settle this issue of God's love. Why?

The best sword in the world won't defeat one enemy if the person wielding it isn't engaged in battle. And prayer is how we "engage." Without prayer, we are as the Israelite army was when they stood on a mountain facing Goliath and the Philistine army—"all dressed up with nowhere to go."

Day after day, Goliath, the champion of Gath, hurled insults at

God's chosen people and defied them to send him a man to engage him in battle. The Bible records that the armies of Israel were set "in array" (1 Samuel 17:21, KJV). They were dressed for battle, lined up for battle, but no one moved. "They were dismayed, and greatly afraid" (verse 11, KJV).

And if we as God's chosen people don't respond to His call to prayer, we, too, will become a pathetic picture of impotence against the burning insults and accusations of the enemy. We, too, will stand there in our spiritual combat fatigues with night-vision goggles and laser-scoped M-16 rifles, arrayed for battle but "dismayed, and greatly afraid."

Are you dismayed about your relationship with God? Is your walk with Him characterized by fear or faith? Will you continue to stand there armed with doctrines, texts, and information that you've absorbed over the years in your head but not in your heart and allow Satan to tell you that you are too great a sinner for God to save? Will you stand there arrayed for battle in religious regalia, only to be pounded with accusations of your own unworthiness, failure, and unacceptableness to God?

"If *my people* . . . pray, . . . I . . . will forgive . . . and will heal" (2 Chronicles 7:14). Go to your knees and wield the sword of God against the enemy. *Learn to confront each false belief with a specific truth from God's Word.* Send Satan's lies back to the pit where they came from, and rejoice in the truth that you have found favor with God. That you are His and He is yours.

Treasured possessions

To be God's people also means that we are His treasured possessions.

"You are a people holy to the Lord your God. Out of all the peoples on the face of the earth, the Lord has chosen you to be his *treasured possession*" (Deuteronomy 14:2, emphasis mine).

We're Family

"And the Lord has declared this day that you are his people, his *treasured possession* as he promised, and that you are to keep all his commands. He has declared that he will set you in praise, fame and honor high above all the nations he has made and that you will be a people holy to the Lord your God" (Deuteronomy 26:18, 19, emphasis mine).

Friends

"You are my friends if you do what I command. I no longer call you servants, because a servant does not know his master's business. Instead, I have called you friends" (John 15:14, 15).

Not only are we children and treasured possessions, but we are God's friends, as well. We are invited to share in the most intimate of relationships with the sovereign Lord and Creator of the universe. He permits me, no, begs me, to know Him as a *Friend*. And we are friends *If* (there's that two-letter word again) we do what He commands.

"Oh no," I can hear some saying. "I knew sooner or later the obedience thing would come up. Does every conversation about God have to involve commandments and obedience?" You bet. Let's get one thing clear. *Jesus* is Lord, not you and certainly not me. That means He's the boss. I'm subject unto Him and His authority in my life. I'm not my own; I've been bought with a price (see 1 Corinthians 6:20), and I now live, not for my own pleasure, but for His.

Does this trouble you? Do you see a contradiction between the necessity of obedience and being God's friend?

One Friday evening not long ago, my middle daughter Crystal was sitting at the dining table with her coat on, preparing to go with the rest of the family to choir rehearsal. A cold had left me with a mild case of laryngitis, so I was remaining behind.

As she waited for the others to get ready, she filled the time by coloring in one of her many Bible-story coloring books, and for some reason that I still haven't figured out, this vivacious five-year-old was contemplating government as she worked. She looked up from her creation and said, "Dad, are you a government?" I paused for a moment, trying to determine where she was headed with this line of questioning. (*With Crystal, you never know!*) I thought maybe I should give some profound answer like, "Sure, the government of my home," but I decided not to.

"No," I said simply, bracing myself for the inevitable follow-up question.

"Why not?" She could be brutal.

"Well, governments are rulers and leaders of this country and of the city and of the state."

She thought about that for a moment and said, "Oh, well, I wish you were a government." Now things were starting to swing in my favor.

"Why is that?" I said, thinking that perhaps she was about to pay me a compliment by saying that I'd be a wise and good ruler, that I would run things well. As I waited for these and other praises, she surprised me by saying, "Because then Candi and I could do whatever we want to."

Shocked, I said, "Oh yeah? That's what you think?"

"Sure. Everybody else would have to obey, but we wouldn't have to."

It suddenly struck me that this is the way many Christians relate to God. They feel that their status as children somehow entitles them to be "above the law." That their "inside track" somehow exempts them from obedience. (This is known as "cheap grace.")

I like to think that our relationship to the Father is similar to the relationship that was shared by Robert and John Kennedy. The two men were brothers and bonded by blood. Theirs was a special relationship. Bobby, as attorney general, was clearly subservient to his brother John. John was his commander in chief, and Bobby was subject to John's authority. Yet because of their special bond and relationship as brothers, Bobby was also acknowledged as the President's closest advisor. He was often taken into John's confidence, and the two men shared many thoughts and ideas about the running of the country.

It wasn't a demeaning subservience, nor was John's position lorded over his brother. They were fulfilling roles in government, one clearly in submission to the other. But it was also a relationship that allowed Bobby access to the inner chambers of the world seat of power.

As God's children today, we are at once servants, friends, brothers and sisters, children, heirs, colaborers, priests, and kings. But Christ is still our head. We are still subject unto Him. We come under His rulership, management, and care for our lives. At the same time, we have unrestricted access into the throne room of the universe, to be loved, nurtured, and taken into the confidence of the Almighty. We obey, not in order to be loved, but because we are loved.

Recipients of mercy

"You are a chosen people, a royal priesthood, a holy nation, a people belonging to God, that you may declare the praises of him who called you out of darkness into his wonderful light. Once you were not a people, but now you are the people of God; once you had not received mercy, *but now you have received mercy*" (1 Peter 2:9, 10, emphasis mine).

Claim it now. You are God's. And it is to you He speaks in 2 Chronicles 7:14. "If *my people* . . ." Can you hear His call just now? It is to His children, His redeemed ones, His treasured possessions, His friends, His chosen ones that He speaks.

We are "His people." And instead of frozen images captured on the pages of some galactic photo album, our faces, our names, our questions and doubts, our triumphs and tragedies, our scars and our warts are tattooed forever onto the palms of God's hands (see Isaiah 49:16).

What does God see when He looks into the hollow of His hand for the folds of flesh that bear our image? I pray He sees a beloved child who is secure in His everlasting love and eager to "share in the very being of God" (2 Peter 1:4, NEB).

Let go of the baloney

In his now-out-of-print book *Come Share the Being,* Bob Benson relates an illustration of what it means to share with God that will stick with me forever.

Do you remember when they had old-fashioned Sunday school picnics? It was before air-conditioning. They said, "We'll meet at Sycamore Lodge in Shelby Park at 4:30 Saturday. You bring your supper and we'll furnish the tea."

But you came home at the last minute and when you got ready to pack your lunch, all you could find in the refrigerator was one dried up piece of baloney and just enough mustard in the bottom of the jar so that you got it all over your knuckles trying to get to it. And there were just two stale pieces of bread. So you made your baloney sandwich and wrapped it in some brown bag and went to the picnic.

And when it came time to eat you sat at the end of a table and spread out your sandwich. But the folks next to you—the lady was a good cook and she had worked all day and she had fried chicken, and baked beans, and potato salad, and homemade rolls, and sliced tomatoes, and pickles, and olives, and celery, and topped it off with two big homemade chocolate pies.

And they spread it all out beside you and there you were with your baloney sandwich.

But they said to you, "Why don't we put it all together?"

"No, I couldn't do that, I just couldn't even think of it," you murmured embarrassedly.

"Oh, come on, there's plenty of chicken and plenty of pie, and plenty of everything—and we just love baloney sandwiches. Let's just put it all together."

And so you did and there you sat—eating like a king when you came like a pauper.

And I get to thinking—I think of me "sharing" with God. When I think of how little I bring, and how much He brings and that He invites me to "share," I know I should be shouting to the housetops, but I am so filled with awe and wonder that I can hardly be heard.

I know you don't have enough love or faith, or grace, or mercy or wisdom—there's just not enough to you. But He has—He has all those things in abundance and says, "Let's just put it all together."

Consecration, denial, sacrifice, commitment, crosses—these were kind of hard, flinty words to me, until I saw it in the light of "sharing." Not just me kicking in what I have because God is the biggest kid in the neighborhood and wants it all for Himself. But He is speaking to me and saying, "Everything that I possess is available to you. Everything that I am and can be to a person, I will be to you."

When I think about it like that, it really amuses me to see somebody running along through life hanging on to their dumb bag with that stale baloney sandwich in it, saying, "God's not to get my sandwich! No sirree, this is mine!" Did you ever see anybody like that—so needy—just about half-starved to death, hanging on for dear life. It's not that He needs your sandwich—the fact is, you need His chicken.[1]

Are you, through prayerlessness, clinging to a stale baloney sandwich, when God is offering you the opportunity to feast on His abundance? Everything that He possesses—"every spiritual blessing in Christ" (Ephesians 1:3)—is available, right now, to you. And it is available through prayer. Won't you come to the Lord's "picnic"? There's always room for family—and that means you. Come share the being. Live no longer as a pauper. You're a child of the King!

---

1. Bob Benson, *Come Share the Being* (Nashville: Impact Books, 1974; Grand Rapids, Mich.: Zondervan, 1982), 105, 106.

Part 3

Called by my name

"The name of the Lord is a strong tower;
the righteous run to it and are safe."
—Proverbs 18:10

"The only place we can hide from God's presence
is in His presence."

Real prayer happens when we respond to God's
call to bear and possess His name.

CHAPTER
6

People of the Name

My wedding day was memorable in many ways. There was the usual excitement that everyone taking this life-changing step experiences. The arrival of the guests, the preceremony photography session, the late-arriving musicians, the water heater that inexplicably blew the closet door nearly off its hinges and narrowly missed maiming my best man and little cousin as they walked past. You know, the usual.

But of everything that happened in that blur of a ceremony, the goose bumps skittered up and down my spine fastest when our pastor introduced us to the world as "Mr. and Mrs. Randyle Maxwell." Spontaneous applause errupted, the organist opened up the pipes with a spirited rendition of "Joy to the World" (it was a Christmas wedding), and as I took Suzette's hand in mine, the smile on my face nearly encircled my head as we walked down the aisle husband and wife.

Something mysterious and wonderful had taken place in the thirty or so minutes it took to perform that ceremony. Suzette Marie Owens became Suzette Marie Maxwell. *She took my name!* Of her own free will, she chose to enter into a relationship with me that spiritually and legally linked her identity with mine.

I had publicly and before God pledged myself to someone I loved. And that someone had done the same for me. In so doing, she loved me enough to surrender something that had been a foundational part of her life since birth—her name.

A name is the most basic element of a person's identity. Your name establishes who you are and where you fit in the human family. It establishes your placement on the family tree and gives you geographical, historical, and relational roots. Few things are as personal as your name. And yet it was this part of herself that she willingly laid aside in order to take on my own.

Sharing a name means sharing a life. My people became her people—and vice versa. My concerns, needs, dreams, and plans became *our* concerns, needs, dreams, and plans. Two had become one, and, though our individuality remains intact, we are identified by the same binding tie—my name.

What's in a name?

Before our third daughter was born, I became obsessed with finding just the right name for her. I went to the local library and returned with stacks of books covering the science of naming from every conceivable angle. I learned which names were "in" and which names were "out." Which names were most likely to help a child get A's in grade school and which names would cause the teacher to assume the child was a dullard and doom him or her to academic obscurity. There were names that would look nice "on the cover of a Broadway playbill" and names that would be most likely to appear on an episode of "America's Most Wanted."

It became a game with me after a while, and soon I was telling my friends and co-workers what their names meant, their origins, and their likelihood of achieving fame, love, and success. OK. I admit I went a little over the top, but it was fascinating.

After making a chart comparing the positives and negatives, meanings, and "energy levels" of our favorite names, we sat in the hospital birthing room cradling our newest miracle (actually, I was sitting; Suzette was flat on her back!) and couldn't decide what to put on the birth certificate! Solomon was right when he said, "With much wisdom comes much sorrow; the more knowledge, the more grief" (Ecclesiastes 1:18). All the stuff I had learned about names was causing my mind to cramp up, and with the pen in one hand and the birth certificate in the other, I was momentarily paralyzed with the fear of branding my child for life.

Suzette wasn't much help. She was just glad the baby was out! Eventually, though, we agreed on the name Danielle Simone, which means "God is my Judge" and "heard by the Lord." Two sentiments that we desire to be a reality for our daughter. When she prays, she can know that she is "heard" by Someone who loves her with an everlasting love and knew her name long before she was born (see Jeremiah 31:3; Psalm 139:13-16). And one day, when she appears before the judgment seat of Christ, she'll know that the God who pleads her case is also her Judge. And there's no need to fear when you have a "Friend in court" (see Romans 14:10; John 5:22).

My own name, Randyle (a modern form of the Old English Randolf—made more modern by the quaint spelling my grandmother gave it), means "shield-wolf." I have no idea what this is. I prefer the spiritual meaning given on those wallet-sized cards you get from the Christian bookstore. I have one that says *Randy* means "protected." Whether or not it really means that, I appreciate the idea that my name carries the connotation of being protected by God.

What's in a name? In Bible times a name was who you were or

what you were going to be. Jacob, "supplanter" (you and I would say "hustler"), lived up to his name and snookered his brother Esau out of a birthright. David, "beloved," was Israel's greatest and most-loved king. He was also the "apple of God's eye." And the wife of Phinehas, upon hearing the news that her husband and father-in-law (Eli) were dead and that the ark of God had been captured, went into labor and gave birth to a son. As she herself lay dying, she named the boy Ichabod, or "no glory," saying, "The glory has departed from Israel, for the ark of God has been captured" (1 Samuel 4:22). Imagine what it must have been like for little "Ichy" in grade school!

A name carries traditions, character traits, and attributes that define who you are and helps reveal something of your origins and where you came from.

Called by God's name

God has a name too. In fact, He has many names.

When God showed Moses how to turn the bitter waters sweet, He made a promise to Israel, saying, "I will not bring on you any of the diseases I brought on the Egyptians, for I am [*Jehova-ropheka*, 'Jehovah who heals you']" (Exodus 15:26).

When He established the Sabbath as a covenant between Israel and Himself, God told Moses, "Say to the Israelites, 'You must observe my Sabbaths. This will be a sign between me and you for the generations to come, so you may know that I am [*Jehovah-meqaddeshkem*, "Jehovah who sanctifieth you"]' " (Exodus 31:13).

David knew Him as *Jehovah-roi*, "Jehovah, my Shepherd," and penned a love poem that immortalizes God's unceasing provision with the words, "The Lord is my shepherd; I shall not want" (Psalm 23:1, KJV).

As Abraham clutched his beloved Isaac to his breast, moments after coming within inches of taking the boy's life in obedience to

God's command, the trembling patriarch spotted a ram entangled in a nearby thicket and called that place *Jehovah-Jireh*, "Jehovah will provide" (Genesis 22:14).

Jehovah-Nissi, "Jehovah is my banner," was the name given by Moses to the altar he built as a memorial of Israel's victory over the Amalekites (Exodus 17:15). And when Gideon trembled after realizing he had been in the presence of the Lord, Jesus came to him and said, "'Peace! Do not be afraid. You are not going to die.' So Gideon built an altar to the Lord there and called it [*Jehovah-shalom*, 'Jehovah is peace']" (Judges 6:23, 24).

These names of God describe who He is—His character and His attributes. And it is by His name, with all its meanings, that He calls you and me.

What exactly does this mean?

It means, first of all, that *God has chosen you to represent His name before the world*. When you publicly declared your love for and allegiance to Christ—whether standing beneath a canvass tent with the sweet smell of sawdust in your nostrils or waist-deep in an icy river or in a baptismal tank framed by a stained-glass mural with the beaming faces of family members looking on from the congregation—and emerged from the waters of baptism, you took His name as your own.

You took the torch of salvation passed on from a long line of followers of "the name" and received the commission from God to bear that name before the world. We are the Lord's witnesses (see Acts 1:8), and as such we represent His healing power before a sin-sick world, for He is *Jehovah-ropheka*—"the God who heals." We reach out to the homeless and hurting and let those in need know *Jehovah-Jireh*—"the Lord provides." And to those whose lives are tortured with the guilt of broken vows, abusive pasts, ruined relationships, and rejected grace, we declare *Jehovah-shalom*—"Jehovah is peace," and *Jesus*—"Jehovah saves!"

Praying in the name

What a privilege not only to represent that name, but to pray in that name.

Jesus said, "I tell you the truth, anyone who has faith in me will do what I have been doing. He will do even greater things than these, because I am going to the Father. And I will do whatever you ask in my name, so that the Son may bring glory to the Father. You may ask me for anything in my name, and I will do it" (John 14:12-14).

Many Christians have seized these words and taken them to mean that God is locked in by His own words to supply them "whatever" they ask, simply by adding the phrase "in Jesus' name" to the end of their prayers. Their attempts have often resulted in disappointment because of a misunderstanding of what Jesus said. To pray in Jesus' name is to ask for things consistent with who He is and what He's about.

> The Lord gave the wonderful promise of the free use of His Name with the Father in conjunction with *doing His works.* The disciple who lives only for Jesus' work and Kingdom, for His will and honor, will be given the power to appropriate the promise. Anyone grasping the promise only when he wants something very special for himself will be disappointed, because he is making Jesus the servant of his own comfort.[1]

Requests that will result in provision, protection, healing, sanctification, peace, and salvation are consistent with the character and name of Christ. We are "called" to represent that name before heaven and earth in our lives and on our knees.

Another meaning

To be called by God's name also means *to be referred to by that name.* God literally gives us His name.

When Suzette became my wife, I no longer referred to her as Suzette Owens. She took my name, and from that moment to this, I've called her by it—Suzette Maxwell—which, incidentally, is now her name. She possesses it fully and all the "rights and privileges" that go along with it.

Though it's hard to believe and should be said with the utmost reverence, God has given us His name. From the moment we accepted Him as our Saviour, He has called us by His holy name—which, incidentally, is now ours.

We were once "supplanters" and "Ichabods," deceivers and symbols of lost glory. But He reached down and called us *Hephzibah*—"My delight is in you" (Isaiah 62:4). We once were strangers and alienated from God, but He has redeemed us. "I have summoned you by name; you are mine" (Isaiah 43:1).

As Suzette fully possesses my name, we fully possess God's name and all the "rights and privileges" that go with it. What are those rights and privileges? The right to belong to His family and the privilege of walking in His presence.

In one of the most moving scenes in the Old Testament, Moses demands to see God's glory, and God grants his wish.

"Moses said to the Lord, 'You have been telling me, "Lead these people," but you have not let me know whom you will send with me. You have said, "I know you by name and you have found favor with me." If you are pleased with me, teach me your ways so I may know you and continue to find favor with you. Remember that this nation is your people.'

"The Lord replied, 'My Presence will go with you, and I will give you rest' " (Exodus 33:12-14).

But Moses wasn't satisfied. He needed more assurance that God was with him. And, as if he hadn't heard what God had said, "Moses said to him, 'If your Presence does not go with us, do not send us up from here. How will anyone know that you are pleased with me and with your people unless you go with us? What else will distinguish me and your people from all the other people on the face of the earth?'

"And the Lord said to Moses, 'I will do the very thing you have asked, because I am pleased with you and I know you by name' " (verses 15-17).

Assured of God's favor, Moses now dared to press his advantage to the limit and make a bold request. "Then Moses said, 'Now show me your glory' " (verse 18).

No lightning bolts zinged from the clouds above to strike this audacious sinner who dared to make such a request. Why should there have been? This was no stranger, no enemy. Moses was God's friend—kinfolk called by His name.

"And the Lord said, 'I will cause all my goodness to pass in front of you, and I will proclaim my name, the Lord, in your presence' " (verse 19).

God knew that Moses couldn't see His face and live, so He put Moses in the cleft of a rock and covered the opening with His hand. Then, as He walked past, He took His hand away so Moses could see His back.

"And he passed in front of Moses, proclaiming, 'The Lord, the Lord, the compassionate and gracious God, slow to anger, abounding in love and faithfulness, maintaining love to thousands, and forgiving wickedness, rebellion and sin' " (34:6, 7).

Did you notice something? The Lord equated all His "goodness" with His name. And when God proclaimed His name to Moses, what did He say? "I am Jehovah, the self-existent, eternal One, the compassionate and gracious God, slow to anger, abounding in love and faithfulness, maintaining love to thousands, and forgiving wickedness, rebellion and sin."

What a God! What a name! Is it any wonder that Solomon says, "The name of the Lord is a strong tower; the righteous run to it and are safe" (Proverbs 18:10)?

Great seas have parted at the mention of that name. With that name the flames of a fiery furnace have been cooled, the jaws of ravenous lions have been shut, cities have been reduced to rubble, and mighty armies have been routed. That name has terrorized demons; hushed a savage storm; brought sight to empty eyes; restored muscle, sinew, and ligaments to useless limbs; vanquished raging fevers from perspiration-soaked brows; and raised the dead. It is a name "above every name," and at its mention, "every knee should bow, in heaven and on earth and under the earth, and every tongue confess that Jesus Christ is Lord" (Philippians 2:9, 10).

And it is by *this* name we are called. Oh, if we only realized and lived up to our privileges as sons and daughters of God—as people of *the name!*

The Lord's name is His glory. And, like Moses, through prayer, you and I can and must ask for God to reveal and cover us with His "glory." And because God is eager to share Himself with His people, He gives us that name, and we are enfolded by His "goodness," branded with the "glory" of His compassion and grace. The call to prayer is a call to first receive and then reveal God's glory—to experience and live in His awesome presence. It is not the voice of a stranger or enemy who calls. Rather, it is the voice of One who knew and loved us with an everlasting love long before we were born (Psalm 139:13-16); One who provides, redeems, heals, sanctifies, shepherds, and saves. One who paid with His life to give us His name.

Bear that name with pride, representing it before the world in everything you say and do. Possess that name fully as your own, and with it—in prayer—open the windows of heaven.

Blessed be the name of the Lord!

---

1. Andrew Murray, *With Christ in the School of Prayer* (Springdale, Penn.: Whitaker House, 1981), 143.

Part 4

Will humble themselves

"Humble yourselves in the sight of the Lord,
and he shall lift you up."
—James 4:10, KJV

"Get down on your knees before the Master;
it's the only way you'll get on your feet."
—James 4:10, The Message

Real prayer places us where we belong—
at the feet of Jesus.

CHAPTER
7

Admitting the Obvious

There was no mistaking it. We were lost. I didn't know when it had happened, but I had missed an exit somewhere, and now we were headed east into the California desert en route to Las Vegas instead of to Lake Arrowhead—our destination for the weekend.

My wife and I had arranged this little getaway to the mountains with our apartment manager, who had a piece of a time-share deal in a Lake Arrowhead condominium. We had use of the place that weekend and had invited friends—two other couples—to come up and enjoy it with us. Our manager had given me the directions to the house, and I felt I had a good grasp on how to get there, even though I'd never been to Lake Arrowhead before.

We left early on Friday so we could be the first ones to arrive. After all, we were the hosts. We should be there to greet our friends. And we also wanted to get settled in before the Sabbath began. Well, we did leave earlier than the others, but not early enough to avoid the weekend traffic out of town.

After I'd stared at a sea of taillights on the 91 freeway for nearly two hours, the flow of traffic began to pick up, and I could finally use my car's third and fourth gears. Soon, however, it became obvious, at least to Suzette, that something was wrong. The signs weren't saying "Lake Arrowhead." They were saying "Las Vegas." And the terrain wasn't getting mountainous; it was getting sandy, flat, desertlike. It was then she suggested getting off the freeway to ask for directions.

Now, men, you know what happened next, don't you? I smiled sweetly at my deluded, but sincere, spouse and said, "Why? We're not lost." Those four little words began a frantic scramble over the California landscape that didn't see us arriving in camp until nearly ten o'clock that night—some three to four hours late!

Yes, I finally stopped for directions—*twice!* And as I punched the accelerator and squeezed the wheel, I fumed at the rutted two-lane road we bumped along, at the car for not going faster, at the sun that refused to stop setting before I could reach our destination. Yes, I fumed at everything but the real culprit in the whole sad affair—me. I wouldn't admit that I had blown it; that I had taken us that much farther out of the way because my pride kept me from pulling off the highway the first time Suzette suggested that there might be a problem.

To top everything off, when we finally arrived, one of the other couples was already there! Sweaty, tense, and cranky, I walked over to their car and began apologizing for being so late. I asked them how they had found the place and how long they had been waiting. The wife beamed a smile and said, "We just got here. We were lost too. But I just prayed and started singing praise songs. I knew we'd get here eventually."

I couldn't have been more stunned if she had slapped my face. What a contrast in behavior! Two couples in two different cars; each lost, each late. In one car, a raving, bug-eyed maniac is lost and angry. In the other car, a praying, praise-singing daughter of God is lost and trusting! *Do you have any idea how crazy that made me?*

I was tired, agitated, demoralized, and rebuked—and I had missed my supper to boot. Humble pie on an empty stomach doesn't go down easily.

Why do we have such a hard time admitting when we've taken a wrong turn? Once we've made up our minds that we're going to pursue a certain course of action, it seems like nothing but disappointing, demoralizing failure can convince us of our error. It's like what happened to my mom and dad on their walk at the nearby recreation center. They were keeping track of their mileage and their time, when my mom mentioned that it was 2:10. "No, it isn't," replied Dad. "My watch says it's 2:15." My mother went on to tell me that despite the fact that *six* other clocks inside the rec center all agreed with her watch, my dad's only response was, "They could be wrong, you know."

A mind, once made up, is a terrible thing to try to change. You can see that in your own life—at home and at work—and you can see it at work in the church. The Lord always has His hands full when He tries to get us back on track—when He points out areas in our lives that desperately need changing. Why is this so hard for God? Because we don't easily admit the obvious—that we *need* to change!

And that's why it is urgent that we understand and hear—really hear—what God is saying to us in 2 Chronicles 7:14.

"If my people." (He's not talking to strangers here. He's talking to you and to me. We are *His;* we belong. He's talking to the sheep of *His* pasture. Not to His enemies but to His friends.)

"Who are called by my name." (Again, we are called by His name. His character, His attributes, and His life are now our life. We share a history—His history; a mission—His mission; and a kingdom—His kingdom. We bear His name and "are therefore Christ's ambas-

sadors, as though God were making his appeal through us" (2 Corinthians 5:20).

"Will humble themselves." Note that this is the first directive in a series of four outlined in this message from God. Before we're told to pray or to seek or to turn, we're told to *humble ourselves.*

Humility begins with listening

It's a sad but true fact about human nature that we seldom listen to reason. We usually turn a deaf ear to a problem until there's a nuclear meltdown, and we're forced to listen.

Think back to the L.A. riots a few years ago. Remember all the media coverage they received? I remember watching Ted Koppel on "Nightline" moderating a town-hall discussion of the issues behind the violence. He also spent time talking with some of the more notorious gang members in the area, getting their perspective on what happened and why.

As I watched, I couldn't help but think what might have happened if all this attention and dialogue had taken place before the riots. If the media moguls and movers and shakers had taken an interest in L.A.'s inner-city turmoil *before* Reginald Denny was pulled from his truck and savagely beaten, would that disgraceful scene ever have happened? Who knows?

The tragic reality is, however, that it took chaos, mayhem, and bloodshed to arrest the attention of America. It took a riot to get people to hear and listen to the cries of a segment of our society that is overlooked and too often ignored.

Of course, by now, the L.A. riots are old news. The media moves on to the next ratings-boosting crisis, and with it go the ears and hearts of America. Are the problems in inner-city Los Angeles resolved? Do the cries continue? Who is listening now? Where are Ted Koppel and the town-hall meetings today?

But as I said, this situation is not unique. We humans often don't listen until it's too late. Why? Because we seldom like what we hear—especially if what we hear challenges us to change an opinion, a way of life, an attitude, or a behavior.

Take, for instance, God's message to the Laodiceans in Revelation 3. We don't really care to hear that we are "pitiful, poor, blind and naked." It doesn't sit well with how we choose to see ourselves. We're well educated; many of us live in fine homes, own several cars, and have good jobs. Spiritually, we may be a little dry, but we have "the truth"—so we've got it made. We know this message is supposed to apply to our church, but mostly it's for all those "other" Adventists who don't have their acts together.

This reminds me of a story that's been told about Kaiser Wilhelm, who, after hearing an explanation of the prophecy in Daniel 2, replied, "I can't accept it. It doesn't fit in with my plans!" Kaiser Wilhelm, did not "humble himself" before God and *listen*. He had other plans. Another agenda. How about you? Are you listening to what God is saying? Does His call to prayer fit in with your plans?

Humility involves submission

I did a study on the word *humble* as it appears in 2 Chronicles 7:14. The Hebrew word used here is *kâna'* (*kaw-nah'*). It means "to bend the knee; to humiliate, vanquish;—bring down (low), into subjection, under, humble (self), subdue." The idea is to bow in submission to a greater authority—to subdue or vanquish one's pride, plans, and self, so that total allegiance can be given to Another.

Isn't it interesting that *kâna'* means to "*bend* the knee"? Especially when what follows next is the directive to pray? Could it be that the very act of praying involves a humbling of ourselves? Kneeling places us in the position of submission, where our egos, attitudes, and agendas are purposely put on the back burner so that God's agenda can be given first place. Isn't this what we need most from God? I'd say Yes.

Following are case histories of individuals who humbled (*kâna'*) themselves before God and what happened as a result. Pay close attention to what their humility looked like.

A tender heart

Exhibit A: King Josiah was in the midst of a major reform movement in Judah. Beginning as a young man of only twenty, he tirelessly waged war against idolatry, toppling the altars of Baal, smashing to bits the Asherah poles and idols above the altars, and burning the very bones of the priests who sacrificed to them.

Six years later, he advanced the reform by rebuilding the temple of God, which had fallen into disrepair during the years of Baal worship. During the renovation, Hilkiah the priest found the Book of the Law amid the ruins and had his secretary Shaphan read it to the king. Notice what happened when Josiah heard the words of God's law.

"When the king heard the words of the Law, he tore his robes" (2 Chronicles 34:19). He immediately inquired of the Lord as to what His words meant. And through the prophetess Huldah, the Lord responded: "Because your heart was responsive [tender] and you . . . *humbled* [*kâna'*] yourself before me and tore your robes and wept in my presence, I have heard you, declares the Lord" (verse 27, emphasis mine).

The action words used to describe Josiah's humility are *tore* and *wept*. But he tore his robes and wept only because he first had a tender heart—a heart that was pliable and open to the Holy Spirit.

Is your heart tender toward God? How do you deal with correction or even reproof? If the truth hits a little too close to home, do you tune out, rankle, and send notes to the pastor "setting him straight" and, in so many words, warning him to "back off"?

God is looking for hearts like Josiah's—hearts that are tender, can be broken, and are responsive to His Spirit. When He finds them, as happened with God's people under Josiah's reign, the covenant is restored and revival begins.

Visible sorrow before God

Exhibit B: Fresh from letting Ben-Hadad, the defeated king of Aram, live and then seizing Naboth's vineyard after his wife Jezebel arranged for Naboth's untimely death, Ahab, king of Israel, was confronted by Elijah. The fiery prophet declared: "'I have found you,' . . . 'because you have sold yourself to do evil in the eyes of the Lord. "I am going to bring disaster on you. I will consume your descendants and cut off from Ahab every last male in Israel—slave or free" ' " (1 Kings 21:20, 21).

A few verses later, the writer of Kings inserts this parenthetical statement about the life of Ahab: "There was never a man like Ahab, who sold himself to do evil in the eyes of the Lord, urged on by Jezebel his wife. He behaved in the vilest manner by going after idols, like the Amorites the Lord drove out before Israel" (verses 25, 26).

And how did Ahab respond to this word from God? "He tore his clothes, put on sackcloth and fasted. He lay in sackcloth and went around meekly." God then came to Elijah and called Ahab's actions *kâna'*. "Have you noticed how Ahab has *humbled* [*kâna'*] himself before me? Because he has *humbled* himself, *I will not bring this disaster in his day*" (verse 29, emphasis mine).

Did you see that? Despite Ahab's wickedness, when he humbled himself before God and visibly demonstrated his sorrow for his sin, God spared Ahab from seeing the fruit of his rebellion.

What point am I trying to make with this illustration? Am I saying that in order for us to humble ourselves today we need to rip our clothes, acquire burlap ponchos, and walk with bowed heads, gazing at the floor? No. The new covenant invites us to "confess our sins," and Jesus is "faithful and just and will forgive us our sins and purify us from all unrighteousness" (1 John 1:9).

However, I do feel there is benefit to expressing sorrow for sin on our knees before God. Bill Hybels, pastor of Willow Creek Community Church and author of *Too Busy Not to Pray*, has said that confession is probably the most neglected area in personal prayer today.[1] We too often gloss over this part of our prayer time and ask for general forgiveness for unspecified, general failure.

But humility before God involves expressing sorrow and remorse for those thoughts and actions that bring dishonor to Him and His kingdom. If you would humble (*kâna'*) yourself before God, admit your mistakes, and be specific, telling God how your sin brought dishonor to Him and hurt your witness to the people involved.

I often write out my prayers in a journal. I've done this for years, because, for me, writing seems to help me focus my thoughts and keep them from wandering. My journal contains a wide range of experiences, emotions, joys, and struggles. Part of the journal entry dated 12/28/93 reads like this:

Lord, I struggle with my lips. Too often I indulge in unflattering talk about another in Your family. I harbor secret contempt for certain people—and I beg Your forgiveness. Replace any malice I may feel with Your compassion, and set a watch over my lips.

Being specific and honest about our sins keeps us from glossing over the truth about ourselves and prevents us from taking sin lightly. Again I agree with Bill Hybels, who says, "About the fifth day in a row that you have to call yourself a liar, a greedy person, a manipulator or whatever, you say to yourself, 'I'm tired of admitting that. With God's power, I've got to root it out of my life.' "[2]

Once this is done, you may then feel free to move on in your prayer, knowing that Jesus has forgiven you and cast that sin into the bottom of the sea (see Micah 7:19).

Admitting the Obvious

Accepting God's discipline

Exhibit C: While Moses was on Sinai, the Lord spelled out the results of obedience and disobedience for the children of Israel. The results of rebellion are not at all pleasant, but despite some fairly heavy talk, the Lord once again revealed His eagerness to show compassion with these words: "If then their uncircumcised hearts be *humbled* [kânaʻ], and they then *accept of the punishment* of their iniquity: Then will I remember my covenant with Jacob, and also my covenant with Isaac, and also my covenant with Abraham will I remember; and I will remember the land" (Leviticus 26:41, 42, KJV, emphasis mine).

No one wants to hear of, let alone deal with, discipline anymore. Granted, there have been abuses in which church members, eager to weed out the "sinners," have demonstrated more the spirit of the vigilante than the Spirit of Christ. But do these abuses indicate that the church is incapable of meting out discipline in a redemptive, Christ-honoring way and consequently must turn its head in the face of open sin? Or that members shouldn't be held accountable to the commandments given by the One they have publicly proclaimed as their Saviour *and Lord?*

I was discussing a hypothetical situation with a co-worker and friend of mine one day while driving to a business luncheon. It was not at all unusual for the two of us to engage in rather spirited discussions about the church, and that day was no exception.

The hypothetical situation involved church members who were involved in an adulterous relationship. The couple's actions were known by many in and outside the church. What role, if any, did the church have in addressing the situation?

My friend assumed a rigid posture and told me that it was none of the church's business. That the church had no authority to butt into the private lives of consenting adults.

Now again, because of abuses we've all seen, many of you readers

77

may be applauding this person's response. But hold on a minute. What, then, are we saying about sin? About the body of Christ? About Christ Himself?

My point here is not to open a discussion on church discipline. Let someone else write that book. I bring it up because God Almighty says that before we can seek Him for revival and a reversal of our current sad condition, we must first *humble* (*kâna'*) ourselves and be willing to admit when we're spiritually out to lunch. That means, despite what my friend said, we must be willing to be led back to Jesus. And that's the point of discipline. Not spite, not revenge, not giving people "what they deserve." (What if we all got exactly what we "deserved"? Humbles you right up, doesn't it?)

The purpose of discipline is to bring us back to God. When we humble ourselves before God, with a tender heart, we acknowledge where we've strayed, reach out for His forgiveness, and submit to His loving discipline, which is meant to repair and restore our damaged relationship.

Until this is done—this attitude of humility demonstrated—all other efforts toward enhanced spirituality must fail. And this is indeed a sad state to be in. To be in open rebellion against God in one aspect of life, while praying for and expecting His blessing in another, is a recipe for despair.

Who's on the throne?

Have you been there? Of course you have. And so have I. There are some things in our lives that we would just as soon keep God away from. Whenever *the* subject or thing is addressed in writing or from the pulpit, we tense, feel the heat rise in our necks, press our lips together so tightly they nearly disappear, and cross our arms in front of us. We refuse to be chastised or challenged on this point by a person or by God, because with this particular thing, we're still sovereign.

Admitting the Obvious

In spite of this resistance, we still expect God to shower us with blessings and answer every prayer. Amazing! If kings of countries—warriors, commanders of armies, royal heads of state—fell on their knees and humbled themselves before the Lord, then who are we, who have no claim to an earthly kingdom, to cling so tightly to the throne?

Remember, Jesus is either Lord of all, or He isn't Lord *at all*. And those He loves, He chastens (see Hebrews 12:6; Revelation 3:19).

Our message of reproof

Personal humility before God for our sins is essential, for it is where personal revival begins. But there is a message of reproof that God sends to His corporate body that must also be responded to with *kâna'*. I touched on it briefly at the beginning of this chapter. Listen to it one more time. (I've chosen to use a contemporary paraphrase of this passage so we could hear it with new ears.)

"I know you inside and out, and find little to my liking. You're not cold, you're not hot—far better to be either cold or hot! You're stale. You're stagnant. You make me want to vomit. You brag, 'I'm rich, I've got it made, I need nothing from anyone,' oblivious that in fact you're a pitiful, blind beggar, threadbare and homeless" (Revelation 3:15, 16, The Message).

And how have we done with this message? Have we, like Josiah, Ahab, Manasseh, and Hezekiah, humbled ourselves before God? Are our hearts tender and accepting of this message of rebuke? Does our self-righteousness and spiritual poverty cause us to weep inside and reach out for God's forgiveness and prescribed remedy? Apparently not.

"Oh, for a religious awakening! The angels of God are going from church to church, doing their duty; and Christ is knocking at the door of your hearts for entrance. But the means that God has devised to awaken the church to a sense of their spiritual destitution *have not been regarded.* The voice of the True Witness has been heard in reproof, but *has not been obeyed.* Men have chosen to follow their own way instead of God's way because *self was not crucified in them.*"[3]

"The testimony of the True Witness has not been *half heeded.* The solemn testimony upon which the destiny of the church hangs has been lightly esteemed, if not entirely disregarded."[4]

As a people, we cannot expect the blessings of revival if we refuse to humble ourselves and bow in submission before the testimony of the True Witness. And what the church must do as a whole, I must first do as an individual before God.

I must get real with God about the thrones in my life that I still occupy. This is tough—no question about it. But that's OK. He's dealt with some pretty tough cases before me. And besides, I'm called by His name. He's on my side—and yours. Isn't it about time we got fully on His?

----

1. Bill Hybels, *Too Busy Not to Pray* (Downers Grove, Ill.: InterVarsity Press, 1988), 53.

2. Ibid., 56.

3. *Testimonies for the Church*, 5:719, 720, emphasis mine.

4. Ibid., 1:181, emphasis mine.

CHAPTER
8

The Foolishness of God

The sign was crude, but the message was clear. Someone had drawn the figure of a person with head bowed and hands clasped, obviously at prayer. The next frame showed the same person in the same praying position; only this time the person was slumped and older. In the last frame, a skeleton sprawled on the table. The caption read: *"Why pray and wait for God to solve your problems?"*

I came across this poster as I walked across the campus of Boise State University, where I was taking some courses. I can't remember now what was being advertised, but I do recall that it was put there by an atheistic group on campus who obviously didn't think highly of prayer. It was "foolishness" to them.

I've done some things in my life that I'm sure appeared foolish to some. I'll never forget the day our church choir sang in "Sherm Alley"—at that time one of the most drug-infested, deadly stretches of asphalt in Los Angeles.

It was during the early eighties, and the drug of choice on the streets was PCP or "Sherm"—if you prefer its street name. In a section of town dubbed "the jungle" was an alleyway between apartment houses that was notorious for the heavy trafficking of this drug. The devil had claimed this piece of California real estate for his own, and most people with good sense stayed away. Most people, that is, except a young Adventist preacher and the members of the Maranatha Seventh-day Adventist Ensemble.

God had put it in the heart of this renegade preacher to invade enemy territory and take some light where it was darkest. The preacher had connections with KDAY, one of the most popular Black radio stations in L.A., and the station agreed to send a large mobile unit to Sherm Alley and broadcast the "worship" service live. My dad, who directed the ensemble, agreed to provide a gospel concert and support the preaching of the Word.

What a sight to behold! There on the oil-stained blacktop of Sherm Alley, in the shadow of high-powered assault weapons held at the ready by L.A.P.D. sharpshooters positioned on the apartment rooftops above us, we sang songs to the glory of God! With a radio-station van, a preacher with a Bible, and a choir, God brought some light to "the jungle." We went onto Satan's turf, stood toe to toe with the enemy, and he blinked. (*We* couldn't blink! Our eyes were wide in abject terror!)

For the first time in what must have seemed like years, the residents of Sherm Alley actually had the courage to walk into the street and listen to words of comfort, hope, and love. For the hour or two we were there, no drugs were dealt, no shots were fired. To some who looked on—our police protectors included—what we were doing out there must have appeared foolish. (As I look back on this now, I'm inclined to agree with them!) "But God hath chosen the foolish things of the world to confound the wise; and God hath chosen the weak things of the world to confound the things which are mighty" (1 Corinthians 1:27, KJV).

The Foolishness of God

The foolishness of prayer

Does prayer seem foolish to you sometimes? I think if we're honest, we'll admit that there are times when prayer seems weak and ineffective. We pour out our souls to God with eloquence and passion; maybe we even throw in a little fasting just to show God how serious we are. We get others to agree with us in prayer and claim every related promise, yet without result. Nothing seems to change. And eventually we get off our knees, feeling rather foolish for having wasted precious time, and look for a way to deal with the problem ourselves.

We've all felt the sting of unanswered prayer. I felt it acutely at my mother-in-law's funeral. For five years, from the time she was diagnosed, I had pleaded with God to heal her. My journal records some of my prayers to God on her behalf. I was eloquent. I presented strong, solid arguments as to why I felt she was a candidate for healing. I knew God didn't say Yes to every prayer for healing, but I begged Him to let her be an exception. I knew some people were healed miraculously. It *does* happen. I asked if she could be one of these.

I was more than a little shocked when she died. I thought God could have been best glorified by healing her. But despite my eloquence, arguments, and passion, the answer was No.

So why pray? The result often seems so arbitrary. Sometimes we win; sometimes we lose. We get some prayers answered, but some we don't. And if God knows what we need before we can ask Him anyway, why pray? Why not just trust Him to supply what He already knows we need and just take life as it comes?

Are you ready for the answer? I hope so, because it's surprisingly simple. But it's basic to what this book is all about and a key element in humbling ourselves before God. The answer? *Because God asks us to pray!* I'm sorry if that answer offends some of the more sophisticated among us, but that's it.

As weak and foolish as it may sometimes appear to be, *prayer is the divinely appointed means by which we cooperate with God in building and expanding His kingdom.* Yes, He knows what we need before we ask, but He wants us to come to Him and confess our trust in His ability to provide for those needs. (I'll have more to say about this in the next section.)

It is in the coming—responding to the call to prayer—that we humble ourselves and assume the position of greatest power in all the universe—the position of absolute surrender and submission. And like so many of the paradoxes of the kingdom, the way down is the way up. The way to glory is the path of abasement. To live is to die, to gain is to lose, to be weak is to be made strong, and to admit need is to possess the kingdom of heaven.

"*From the soul that feels his need, nothing is withheld. He has unrestricted access* to Him in whom all fullness dwells."[1] In prayer, we put our sophistication on hold and acknowledge that God knows more than we do and that He can do "immeasurably more than all we ask or imagine" (Ephesians 3:20).

Time to do things God's way

God has a way of doing things in an unorthodox fashion. To us, His methods at times seem crude, backward, and illogical. Some might even say "foolish."

When Naaman, the proud Syrian general, came to Elisha, seeking relief from his leprosy, he couldn't believe his ears when Elisha told him to dip seven times in the muddy waters of the Jordan. What a stupid prescription for healing! To this battle-hardened leader of men, this directive must have sounded as backward to him as a voodoo witch doctor's chicken-bone cure would sound to us.

It made no sense! Naaman was already covered with sores. The filthy waters of the Jordan would only swell those sores with infection. Besides, you can't bathe away leprosy! He'd taken many baths—

in *clean* water, no less—without an improvement to his condition. And why seven times? It made no *rational* sense. But Naaman obeyed God's "foolishness," and the record states that "he went down and dipped himself in the Jordan seven times, as the man of God had told him, and his flesh was restored and became clean like that of a young boy" (2 Kings 5:14).

What general drafts a battle plan that calls for the choir to lead the army into war? This is crazier than sending a choir into Sherm Alley. Yet this is what Jehoshaphat did when faced with the vast armies of the Moabites and Ammonites.

Jehoshapat shut down the war room. He canceled the joint-chiefs-of-staff meeting and sent everyone in the Pentagon home early. He shut off the computers and did something that may have appeared foolish to the seasoned war strategist—he prayed. He proclaimed a fast for all Judah, gathered all the people together at the temple of the Lord in Jerusalem, and cried to God with these words: "We have no power to face this vast army that is attacking us. We do not know what to do, but our eyes are upon you" (2 Chronicles 20:12).

The Lord answered Jehoshapat by telling him that the battle was His (verse 15). The men of Judah wouldn't even have to fight. They were simply to take up their positions and watch the Lord defeat the enemy. Jehoshaphat assembled the men the next morning, and before they engaged the enemy, he received a flash of inspiration. "Men," he began. "I want to do something a little different today. God has given us a secret weapon, and if we use it, our success is guaranteed!" Imagine what was going through the minds of those soldiers when Jehoshaphat revealed that the "secret weapon" was the choir!

After consulting the people, Jehoshaphat appointed men to sing to the Lord and to praise him for the splendor of his holiness as they went out at the head of the army, saying: "Give thanks to the Lord, for his love endures forever."

As they began to sing and praise, the Lord set ambushes against the men of Ammon and Moab and Mount Seir who were invading Judah, and they were defeated. The men of Ammon and Moab rose up against the men from Mount Seir to destroy and annihilate them. After they finished slaughtering the men from Seir, they helped to destroy one another.

When the men of Judah came to the place that overlooks the desert and looked toward the vast army, they saw only dead bodies lying on the ground; no one had escaped (2 Chronicles 20:21-24).

The "foolishness" of God.

God loves to use the "foolish" things of this world to confound the wise. He used a shepherd's rod to free a nation of slaves and subdue an empire of might (see Exodus 4). He used the jawbone of an ass in the hands of a Nazarite strong man to slay one thousand of the Philistines' best soldiers (see Judges 15:15). He used a shepherd boy's sling and five smooth stones to bring down a giant who had paralyzed the entire Israelite army with fear (see 1 Samuel 17:40).

And now, this great God of the universe, who does such "foolish" things, asks you and me to humble ourselves and pray. Will we do it? If God had asked us to do some great thing—some very complicated, highly technical evangelism strategy that would revolutionize Christianity as we know it, we'd do it in a heartbeat. But He asks us, instead, like He asked Naaman, to dip seven times in the Jordan. He asks us, instead, to march in silence seven times around Jericho. He asks us, instead, to speak to the rock for water. He asks us to do what often appears weak and illogical and backward. He asks us to pray.

I stood in front of a small group who had assembled on a Thursday night for a special prayer meeting. We had moved our regular midweek prayer service to coincide with the National Day of Prayer, and I had hoped for a good turnout.

Only sixteen showed. *So typical,* I thought to myself, *of prayer meetings in our churches.* With the exception of two or three of us, everyone else was over fifty. We certainly didn't look like a powerful band of prayer warriors preparing to storm the gates of hell. I looked at the group and wondered if we could accomplish anything of significance with our prayers that evening. But God had something to show me.

It happened during the time for prayer requests, as first one and then another began to share stories of conversions and souls won to Christ. Two people were giving Bible studies, and the couple they were studying with were on the verge of making their stand for Christ, but the enemy was holding them back with fears of lost income due to Sabbath observance.

Another person—the most elderly in the bunch—wanted strength to keep up with all the community-service demands placed on her. And by the way, she was responsible for bringing two of the people seated in that very room into the church. Other stories came forth. Of lives changed, souls won, battles being fought daily that escape the notice of most of us.

And then I saw what God wanted to show me. What appeared to be small and frail and weak and insignificant was really more powerful than I could have imagined. Why? Because

God chose the weak things of the world to shame the strong. He chose the lowly things of this world and the despised things— and the things that are not—to nullify the things that are, so that no one may boast before him (1 Corinthians 1:27-29).

The group of sixteen mostly elderly believers didn't have the look or feel of fifty-two thousand candle-bearing men gathered in a Boulder, Colorado, football stadium for a Promise Keepers rally last summer. But it was ground zero for the thermonuclear presence of the living God, because where two or three are gathered together in His name, He's there (see Matthew 18:20)!

Jesus, not we, is the Superstar. He is not limited by our narrow conceptions of what we think is possible. "Nothing can hinder the Lord from saving, whether by many or by few" (1 Samuel 14:6).

It's time we did things God's way. I know it seems at times as if nothing is happening and that prayer is a waste of time. But nothing is ever wasted when we obey God. We may have "fished" all night and taken nothing, but at Jesus' bidding, let's drop our nets on the *right* side of the boat. Let's try His way one more time, pray, and see what happens.

We just may receive more than our puny nets of faith can hold.

Lord, I confess that I have often approached prayer more out of a sense of duty than out of a sincere belief that it would make a real difference. When my conscience convicts me that I should pray, I rush through a set of well-rehearsed phrases to make me feel like I've done my part. But this must stop. I now realize that my own pride and unbelief have kept me from a rich and meaningful prayer life. I see now that what appears weak and foolish to me is what God uses to demonstrate His wisdom and power. Teach me to grasp the "foolishness of God." Help me to humbly seek You in prayer. Move me beyond the rut of pet phrases and pious-sounding words to heart-to-heart communion with You. Meet me on my knees, Jesus, and show me Your glory. I can't make it without You.

---

1. Ellen G. White, *The Desire of Ages* (Boise, Idaho: Pacific Press Publishing Association, 1940), 300.

Before You Continue . . .

I want to pause here and just open my heart to you for a few moments before we continue on our journey. It's important for you to know where I'm coming from as we prepare to confront the heart of this book in the next few chapters.

I've said it earlier in this book, but I feel a need to say it again. I do not consider myself to be a "prayer warrior." When I think of someone who is a prayer warrior, I think of a woman I had the privilege of knowing and working with at my former church in Inglewood, California. Now, there was a person who could pray! Whenever we would pray in a group, even if you felt that your own prayers were bouncing off the ceiling, you just knew that hers "got through." She has the gift of intercession.

I also think of a prayer warrior as someone who places such a premium on communion with God that he or she consistently and purposefully devotes quality and quantity time to be with Him on a daily basis. Prayer is not a hit-and-miss thing with a prayer warrior.

Prayer is life to him, and he's arranged his lifestyle around this priority.

I'm not there yet. But I hear God's call for me toward that goal, and like Paul said:

> By no means do I count myself an expert in all of this, but I've got my eye on the goal, where God is beckoning us onward—to Jesus. I'm off and running, and I'm not turning back (Philippians 3:13, 14, The Message).

And I guess that's what I want to share with you before you read farther.

I'm not writing to you as an expert who is giving you the benefit of my great wisdom and experience. I'm simply attempting to give voice to the call to pray that I'm feeling in my life. I'm a fellow student with you in Christ's school of prayer and am just as challenged by what I write as I pray you are by what you're reading.

I know that you're interested in prayer. Why else would you be reading this book? And many of you already have strong, meaningful prayer lives. My purpose isn't to wow you with some great new teaching on prayer that you've never heard before. With so many excellent titles available on the subject, this would be hard to do. Besides, lack of *teaching* on prayer isn't the problem. Lack of *implementation* is.

God is calling me to give unprecedented priority to seeking His face in prayer. And I believe He's calling you to the same thing. If I didn't believe that with all my heart, I wouldn't be up at 4:30 a.m. writing this. God is calling His church to seek Him with all their hearts, and we *must* respond.

For some of you, prayer is already a way of life. It's a joy and a pleasure for you. For others of you, prayer is boring. You struggle to concentrate, to stay awake, and seldom see any significant results to your efforts.

Stick with me. I don't have all the answers, but God does. "All His biddings are enablings,"[1] and He wouldn't call us if He didn't also plan to show us how to answer.

The second directive of 2 Chronicles 7:14—the directive to pray—lies before us. Let's remove our shoes, for we're about to venture onto holy ground. With the humble heart of the student, let's pull up a chair in Christ's school of prayer and learn how to possess the key to revival and how to experience the deeds of omnipotence.

So let's keep focused on that goal,
those of us who want everything God has for us.
If any of you have something else in mind,
something less than total commitment,
God will clear your blurred vision—you'll see it yet!
Now that we're on the right track,
let's stay on it (Philippians 3:15, 16, The Message).

---

1. *The Desire of Ages*, 827.

Part 5

And pray

"Pray in the Spirit on all occasions with all kinds of prayers and requests. With this in mind, be alert and always keep on praying for all the saints."
—Ephesians 6:18

"Our problem has been that we have thought about prayer, read about prayer and even received teaching regarding prayer, but we just have not prayed. Now is the time to understand that prayer is the source of power."
—Paul Y. Cho

Real prayer changes you, the church, and the world.

And pray

CHAPTER

9

A Passion for Prayer

(Personal)

It's 5:00 a.m. While most sleep, thousands of believers are gathered for an early-morning prayer meeting. They will pray for the better part of two hours before beginning their workday. This is not a special "week of prayer" or a once-a-week occurrence. These seekers are here at 5:00 a.m. every single day, year in and year out.[1]

It's Friday evening. In addition to the earlier daily prayer meeting at 5:00 a.m., passersby are shocked to see the church parking lot full between the hours of 10:00 p.m. and dawn the next day. What's going on? The weekly "all-night" prayer session that, at least in one church, commonly sees ten thousand in attendance.[2] (That was not a misprint—*ten thousand!*)

More than two hundred congregations have purchased mountain property on which they've built prayer retreat centers. At one of the larger centers, it's not uncommon to find three thousand pray-ers Monday through Friday and more than ten thousand on weekends.[3]

Where is this revival of prayer taking place? What compels people by the thousands to spend so much time praying? And what are the results, the effects, of this much prayer?

In order, the answers are: South Korea; a burden for souls; and staggering church growth.

Over the past 100 years, Protestant Christianity has grown from zero to more than 30 percent of the population of South Korea. . . . Of the 20 churches in the world that count weekend attendance of 20,000 or more, 9 of them are in Korea alone. The largest Baptist church, the largest Methodist church, the largest Presbyterian church, the largest holiness church and the largest Pentecostal church in the world are all in Korea. David [formerly know as Paul] Yonggi Cho's Yoido Full Gospel Church is the world's largest, having a membership of 700,000.[4]

The dedication of the Korean Christians to seeking God in prayer is further illustrated in this incident related by Dr. C. Peter Wagner in his book *Churches That Pray.*

While in Korea recently, I visited my good friend Pastor Sundo Kim of the Kwang Lim Methodist Church. This visit was toward the end of a special 40-day "Mount Horeb Prayer Meeting," during which he had called his congregation to special early-morning prayer. Even those who did not ordinarily attend the early-morning prayer meetings were urged to come each morning and pray from 5:00 to 6:00. He told me that attendance had been running between 3,000 and 4,000 each morning.

This I had to see. Pastor Kim agreed to provide transportation. The next morning his driver was to pick up Doris and me at our hotel; but it was not easy. A record-breaking storm engulfed Korea that night and more than 60 lives were lost to its fury. The rain and wind were so ferocious at 5:00 the next morning that I wondered if anyone at all would leave their homes for a prayer meeting. But the driver showed up, we went to the church, and arrived after the meeting started; if someone had not reserved seats for us, we would not have had a place to sit. The 4,000-seat sanctuary was packed! What a prayer meeting![5]

Here in America, we're accustomed to the phenomenon of "fair-weather" Christians. It seems that it doesn't take much in the way of rain, cold, wind, or snow to cut deeply into church attendance. In some cases, as I discovered after a recent poorly attended men's meeting, even *good* weather can spell disaster for spiritual programs. I recall telling someone that I had missed seeing him at the men's rally, to which he replied, "Well, the weather was so great, I decided to spend the day with my family at the park."

What's my point in all this? Am I trying to say that bigger is better? Or that quality is defined by quantity? Not at all. I'm very familiar with this statement by Ellen White:

God would be better pleased to have six truly converted to the truth as a result of their [the ministers'] labors, than to have sixty make a nominal profession, and yet not be thoroughly converted.[6]

No, numbers aren't everything. But from all I've read about these Korean believers, their profession is anything but nominal. I bring up their prayer habits here because I'm more than a little curious to know what brings four thousand Korean believers together for prayer at 5:00 a.m. in the midst of a killer storm and why our typical Adventist prayer gatherings (special "weeks of prayer" included) seem to generate only anemic attendance even in the best weather!

Obviously, to the Korean Christian, prayer is important, effective, and a number-one priority. Commenting on how his church members maintain their commitment to the daily 5:00 a.m. early-morning prayer meetings, Paul Cho states, "Since the most important thing in our lives is prayer, we have learned to retire early."[7]

Amazing! They've arranged their lifestyles around the priority of prayer. We, on the other hand, tend to fit prayer around the priorities of our busy lifestyles. How about it? Is prayer "the most important thing in our lives"? Let me put my own self on the hook here. Is prayer the most important thing in *my* life? Am I that serious about prayer? What would it take to get me out to a 5:00 a.m. prayer meeting scheduled by my local church?

My wife and I asked each other these very questions recently after breakfast one Sunday. I had just finished reading her some of the same stories I've been sharing with you, when she asked me, "What would make you go to an early-morning service like that at our own church?" I confessed that I didn't really know.

After wrestling with the question out loud for a few moments, I decided that I would have to believe that the prayer service would make a difference in my life and that I had a need.

And it is here—at the intersection of belief and need—that my true attitude and your true attitude toward prayer is revealed. Do we really believe that God hears and answers prayer? Are we convinced that prayer makes a difference—that unlimited power is made available to us through prayer? Do we really feel a need for prayer? What is our true attitude concerning this?

What follows are a sampling of attitudes about prayer that keep us off our knees. If the shoe fits, discard it.

Prayer as exercise

Many of us view prayer the same way we do exercise—it's a drag. We know exercise is good for us. It relieves stress, improves the circulation, strengthens the heart, boosts the energy level, and improves physical appearance. Some claim that exercise even enhances one's sex life!

But despite these valid and desirable benefits, many of us would rather keep lifting a fork to our mouths than lift weights. Exercise is boring, painful, and just too much trouble after a hard day sitting on our spreading posteriors down at the air-conditioned office!

It is true, however, that some people actually enjoy exercising. These fitness freaks belong to health clubs, play racquetball, swim laps, run track, lift weights, and ride the Lifecycle Stationary bike. Their hearts and lungs are in great shape. They seem to have endless supplies of energy. They look good and feel good. But we know what their problem is, don't we? They're *fanatics*.

The truth is, we don't feel too bad the way we are. We may not be bouncing off the ceiling, but we're doing OK. And as long as our doctor isn't telling us to start walking or kiss our hearts goodbye, we, and our spare tires, keep rolling along.

Sadly, this is how too many of us view prayer. We know prayer is good. Deep down in our spirits, we know that prayer is important— that it strengthens our relationship with God, relieves stress, boosts our faith, and is the source of unlimited spiritual power.

But despite these valid and desirable benefits, many of us view prayer as boring, painful, and just too much trouble.

Prayer as discipline

Another attitude that must be changed is the one that views prayer as discipline.

This is the eat-your-spinach-because-it's-good-for-you approach to prayer. We pray because "prayer is to the soul what breathing is to the body." You can't do without air, right? Neither can you do without prayer, so the thinking goes. Prayer is a spiritual discipline that will make us grow into strong Christians, and we all know that we lazy, lukewarm, complacent, asleep-at-the-switch Christians need more discipline, right?

So off we go in hot pursuit of the "disciplines" that will turn us into superb pray-ers. We learn how to pray for an hour a day; how to pray through the sanctuary; the proper sequence our prayers should take (i.e., ACTS praying: Adoration, Confession, Thanksgiving, and Supplication); the appropriate posture for prayer (to raise the hands or not to raise the hands—that is the question!); and on and on. In other words, we become so obsessed with the *rules* for praying (an easy thing for Adventists to do) that we soon forget the reason we're praying in the first place and give up in frustration when we aren't "disciplined" enough to maintain our regimen.

Forgive me if I'm overstating my case here. Discipline isn't all bad. The formulas and methods do serve a valuable purpose—they give us a place to start.

In David Winter's *Closer Than a Brother* (a modern-day reinterpretation of *Practicing the Presence of God,* by Brother Lawrence), "Laurie," as Brother Lawrence is referred to in this book, responds to a question about set hours of prayer or "quiet times" like this:

> "Well—yes, I do have set times of prayer, and I believe they are a useful discipline, especially for a beginner . . . a learner, as you might say. . . . Set times of prayer are valuable in order to form a habit of conversation with God, and—as I said—referring all we do to him. They aren't the end itself, but means to an end. The end is God: being with him, living in his presence and under his control."[8]

So the mechanics and formulas give us a place to begin. And many people, myself included, have been blessed and enriched by them.

The danger with this view of prayer, however, is falling into the subtle trap of thinking we've failed to communicate with God on those occasions when our prayers didn't follow the regimen. When we didn't pray in the ACTS sequence or immediately upon waking *before* shaving or showering, or if we prayed for only ten minutes instead of for an hour.

But enough of the negative views of prayer. Let's go back now and try to identify new attitudes that will motivate us to go often and eagerly to our knees.

Prayer as relationship

My wife is my best friend. Everything in my life is better because of her. I enjoy her company, and I hate being separated from her. As I write this, I'm more than six hundred miles from home on a business trip to Denver. I miss her terribly. If she were here, I know we'd be enjoying one of our favorite trivial pursuits—people watching. We'd kibitz about the gaudy duds being worn by the dancers here in the hotel who've come to compete in the "World's II Country Western Dance Championships 1994." We'd hit the malls and, if the kids weren't here, just enjoy *talking* without interruption.

When I come home from work, we often fight the kids off so we can spend the first few moments of our reunion snuggling, catching up on each other's day, and reconnecting after an eleven-hour separation. Yes, I'm proud to say that fifteen years of marriage and three children haven't slowed my heart rate one beat for this woman who shares my name and my life.

Imagine how fast the honeymoon would grind to a screeching halt, however, if I always began and ended a conversation with her in exactly the same way. How long would it take for her to be bored out of her mind with me if I said the *same* thing in the *same* way at the *same* time in the *same* sequence day after day after day?

How absurd! You can't have an enjoyable relationship under these circumstances. With Suzette, I enjoy spontaneity; variety; give and take; long, introspective talks (once or twice a year!); and short, Honey-I-love-yous during the busy day.

If this is how we keep our own human relationships vital and fresh, what makes us think our relationships with God can be kept vital and fresh with the same old prayer day in and day out?

We love variety—so does God! He created us with an unlimited capacity for creative expression. It stands to reason, therefore, that He also has an unlimited capacity for creative expression. (Just look at a peacock, seashell, or platypus if you don't believe me!)

If prayer is boring to you, check your conversation. Are you stuck in a rut, praying the same thing with almost the same words over and over again?

I love what F. Laubach said about this.

> The notion that religion is dull, stupid and sleepy is abhorrent to God, for He has created infinite variety and *He loves to surprise us.* If you are weary of some sleepy form of devotion, probably God is as weary of it as you are. Shake out of it, and approach Him in one of the countless fresh directions.

And Maltbie D. Babcock hit the target when she said, "Our prayers must mean something to us if they are to mean anything to God."[9]

I acknowledge that there are times when we're dealing with circumstances or situations that require perseverance. I'm not talking about these here. God doesn't get weary with our daily pleas for our children or for the healing of a marriage that appears to be over.

No. I'm talking about the kind of praying we do when we put our minds on "cruise" and rattle off pet phrases without even thinking about what we're saying. But even if this is the best we can offer, *God still accepts it and us just as we are.* He just wants us to come.

Begin to view prayer, not as exercise or discipline, but as relationship—sharing life with your best friend.

OK. You agree with me that you need to be more creative. But maybe it's hard for you to come up with new ideas. In the next chapter, we'll address specific "action points" to help you begin practicing prayer as relationship. Let's face it; before we can start looking forward to hour-long, predawn prayer sessions, we should first begin enjoying the times, however brief, that we share with God right now.

1. Paul Y. Cho with R. Whitney Manzano, *Prayer: Key to Revival* (Waco, Tex.: Word Books, 1984), 15.

2. C. Peter Wagner, *Churches That Pray* (Ventura, Calif.: Regal Books, 1993), 25, 26.

3. Ibid., 26.

4. Ibid., 23.

5. Ibid., 24, 25.

6. Ellen G. White, *Evangelism* (Hagerstown, Md.: Review and Herald Publishing Association, 1946), 320.

7. *Prayer: Key to Revival,* 15.

8. David Winter, *Closer Than a Brother* (Wheaton, Ill.: Harold Shaw Publishers, 1971), 38, 39.

9. As quoted in Joni Earickson Tada's *Seeking God: My Journey of Prayer and Praise* (Brentwood, Tenn.: Wolgemuth and Hyatt, Publishers, Inc., 1991), 21.

C H A P T E R

10

More Passion for Prayer
(Personal)

I've got a problem. Maybe you have it too. It's spelled *c-o-n-s-i-s-t-e-n-c-y*. I have the best of intentions, the warmest, fuzziest feelings, but I'm still praying for God to give me the victory over repeatedly hitting the snooze button on my alarm clock most mornings. And yet, I *want* to pray. I *want* to be with Him at the beginning of my day.

But I'm discovering that desire is not enough. I must *choose* to get out of bed and talk to God every day. There are no shortcuts. When it comes to our relationship with Jesus, *choosing* to pray—to be with Him—is often the greatest battle.

Once you've made the choice, however, what can you do to shake yourself out of the doldrums and experience some fresh, new approaches to God in prayer?

Action points for enhancing your personal prayer time

1. *Pray whenever you think about it.* Jesus, in answer to a theological question put to Him by the woman at the well, replied, "A time is coming and has now come when the true worshipers will worship the Father in spirit and truth, for they are the kind of worshipers the Father seeks" (John 4:23).

The Samaritans (and the Jews, for that matter) were hung up on the right *place* to worship. They were sure that the true God could only be approached at the "right" spot. Hence, the Samaritan woman's statement: "Our fathers worshiped on this mountain, but you Jews claim that the place where we must worship is in Jerusalem" (verse 20).

Jesus adjusted her attitude and shifted her paradigm by revealing the truth about God—that He is spirit and not confined by man-made temples or times. God is an ever-present reality all the time, everywhere. And true worshipers of the true God can make contact with Him anytime, anywhere.

Don't make the mistake of thinking you can pray only at certain times and in certain places. *Pray when you think about it.* In your car, in a meeting, in bed when you can't sleep, as you mow the lawn or wash dishes, or while brushing your teeth. Brother Lawrence said this about his "anytime" prayers:

> "God is no nearer to me during my 'quiet time' than he is at this very moment in the kitchen; and prayer is no more real when it is said formally, on my knees by my bed, than when I say it informally over the sink or the oven. I really can't wait until ten at night or seven in the morning to refer some vital matter to God. I need him too much and too often to be able to leave things until a particular hour of the day. And his presence is so real that there is no danger that I'll forget to talk with him if I don't make an appointment with him!"[1]

Learn this if you learn nothing else: Because God makes His home in you (see John 14:23; 1 Corinthians 6:19), *wherever you are, God is!* So learn to converse with Him all the time. Besides, when you think about praying, that's God talking!

The natural man or woman doesn't desire prayer. "You, however, are controlled not by the sinful nature but by the Spirit, if the Spirit of God lives in you" (Romans 8:9). If it's on our minds to pray, it's the Holy Spirit calling. Don't put the King on hold! Answer His page, and hear what's on His mind!

I used to—and still do occasionally—fall into the trap of telling myself, "I'll pray about that later." I'll be mowing the lawn, thinking of someone I need to pray for. I'll mentally review the details of that person's need and even rehearse what I plan to say *later* during my "prayer time." It's then that I catch myself and smile at how foolish it is for me to pray later about something I'm thinking (and actually praying) about *now!*

If you kick yourself for forgetting to pray for people you've promised to pray for, learn to pray when God puts it on your mind—when you think about it.

2. *Pray about a variety of things.* I enjoy talking about the new minivan our family of five so desperately needs and one day will purchase. Suzette and I talk about it a lot these days—especially as we (and the three children) prepare to endure an eleven-hour driving trip in the Jetta later this summer! But this is not all we talk about.

We talk about the kids, schooling, the church, vacation plans, family members, music, bills, romance, TV programs, work, etc. And guess what? We don't try to talk about everything all in one sitting! We pace ourselves. Talking about this now, that later; this thing today, the other thing tomorrow.

Do the same with prayer. Don't pray about the same things all the time, and don't try to cover everything in one prayer. Vary your conversation. Pray about the supervisor who gives you grief today, and save time for the missionaries tomorrow.

Pray different types of prayers. Try praying a prayer of praise without any petitions. Make no requests about anything. Put away the shopping list and just spend time praising God for who He is in your life.

Or sing your prayer to God. Paul admonishes us to "sing psalms, hymns and spiritual songs with gratitude in your hearts to God" (Colossians 3:16). There are times when we pray by singing favorite praise hymns such as "Great Is Thy Faithfulness" or "I Love You, Lord."

During sung prayers, I sometimes experience the presence of God more profoundly than when I'm at my "regular" prayers.

3. *Pray without words.* You don't always have to have something to say in order to be with God. I know this may seem odd to some, but sometimes it's perfectly all right "to be still, and know that [He is] God" (Psalm 46:10).

One morning not long ago, I had a deeply moving encounter with God without saying a word. It was one of those extremely rare times when both the house and my spirit were quiet. I couldn't think of anything to read or anything really to say. I sat in the stillness and just allowed my heart to be an open book to God.

As I sat there with the first rays of dawn spilling onto my office carpet through the tiny slits in the miniblinds, I knew I was in the presence of God. I noted the experience in my journal later that morning.

The stillness of this morning feels good—like a warm blanket on a cold night. I seem unable—or unwilling—to think of a passage to read from the Bible. I'm not in a hurry to read anything. For now, the silence is enough. My thoughts and the quiet seem prayer enough this morning. "Be still [cease striving] and know that I am God," You've said. This is one of those rare moments when I'm content to sit still and know You. To have my soul knit to Yours in the calm of this morning. To connect with the King. Thank You for meeting me here this morning (journal entry, 26 April 1994).

Don't be afraid of silence. In our culture, we drown out silence every chance we get. Nature hates a vacuum, and so do we. We feel compelled to quench quiet with sound. TV, radios, CD players, Walkman stereos, Gameboy video games, our own chatter. On airplanes, while exercising, at the dinner table, in the restroom, and on elevators, we have to have some kind of music, noise, or other auditory distraction grinding away in the background.

Learn to "be still and know." Quiet can be profound. And don't feel like you "fail" if words escape you occasionally when you pray. Remember, there are times when "we do not know what we ought to pray for, but the Spirit himself intercedes for us with groans that words cannot express. And he who searches our hearts knows the mind of the Spirit, because the Spirit intercedes for the saints in accordance with God's will" (Romans 8:26, 27).

4. *Keep your prayer time and Bible-study time separate.* This suggestion may get me in trouble, but it's worth trying. Some of us have been trained to structure our "devotions" with prayer and Bible study. And like our typical midweek "prayer" meetings, the emphasis is heavier on the Bible-study side. (In reality, our midweek prayer meetings should be called what they are: Bible studies.)

It's been my experience that when I bring quarterlies, commentaries, and multiple translations of the Bible into my devotional time, I spend little time in prayer and much more time in study. Please don't put this book down and start a rumor about Randy Maxwell's campaign to eliminate Bible study. Would that we were known as "people of the Book" again! I'm simply suggesting that we give each of these its own time.

Prayer is primarily meeting with God. Reading and studying during this time may not always be required. As I said earlier, whether you're just being quiet with Him or focusing on your own needs, you're still meeting with Him. This is *not* wasted time.

5. *Pray for your spouse.* Not in a general, vague way, but in specific terms, claiming certain Bible promises for him or her that are tailored to individual needs.

I like to do this for Suzette and sometimes will leave her a note with the verse that I'm claiming for her on it. She has saved one of these notes and keeps it on the bathroom mirror, where she can see it every day. It reads:

> For you today: That your delight will be in the law of the Lord, that you will meditate on it day and night. That you will be like a tree planted by streams of water, yielding fruit in season without withering. And that whatever you do will prosper (Psalm 1:2, 3). Love ya.

You love your spouse. He or she has struggles, frustrations, goals, hopes, and needs that you probably know about. Take those things to God in prayer. Lift your husband or wife before the Father, and ask Him to meet his or her needs according to His unfailing love.

Search the Word for specific verses that fit his or her situation, and pray those verses back to God, inserting your spouse's name in the appropriate place. I did this recently for my wife while I was out of town and she was nervously awaiting the results of some medical tests back home. We were both on edge, and I went to the Bible for a word of encouragement from the Lord. I found it in Psalm 33:18-22. I claimed the promise for Suzette and then prayed it back to God something like this:

> Suzette waits in hope for You, Lord; be her help and her shield today. Let her heart rejoice in You and help her to trust in Your holy name. May Your unfailing love rest upon us both, O Lord, even as we put our hope in You (verses 20-22).

Later, I called home and told her I was praying this promise for her. I could tell she was pleased. Nothing brings you closer together as a couple than praying earnestly and specifically for the man or woman who shares your life. (P.S. You can pray for your children the same way.)

And, singles, the absence of a spouse doesn't indicate the absence of other individuals who love you and need your prayers. Claim promises on behalf of your best friend, co-worker, family member, nieces and nephews, or pastor, and let them know that you are praying for them. Any relationship will be strengthened by this prayerful act of love.

6. *Pray (or speak) a blessing on your family members.* Anyone can do this, but I'm going to talk to the men reading this right now.

In the sixth chapter of Numbers, we come across the priestly blessing that Aaron and his sons were instructed to bless the Israelites with. Read these words with me carefully:

> The Lord said to Moses, "Tell Aaron and his sons, 'This is how you are to bless the Israelites. Say to them: "The Lord bless you and keep you; the Lord make his face shine upon you and be gracious to you; the Lord turn his face toward you and give you peace." *So they will put my name on the Israelites, and I will*

bless them' " (Numbers 6:22-27, emphasis mine).

Did you see that last part? God said that the priests—Aaron and his sons, in this case—were to put the Lord's name (the promises that are inherent in His attributes, His nature, and His character) on the children of Israel by speaking these words of blessing. What father or mother wouldn't want this blessing to be on their children?

As recipients of the new covenant, we who have received Christ as our Saviour are part of a new breed of humans on earth. Regardless of race or gender, we have been made into "a chosen people, *a royal priesthood*, a holy nation, a people belonging to God" (1 Peter 2:9, emphasis mine). Additionally, we are the spiritual children of Abraham, inheritors of the promises to Israel. These two facts provide us with the commission, qualification, and authority to bless, as priests under the old covenant did.

Like Abraham, we are to be channels through whom God will provide, protect, and profusely spread His blessing. Men (and caregivers), as priests of our homes, God wants us to transmit that blessing to the children.

My wife and I have done this together. With our hands placed gently on the heads of our girls, I've prayed this blessing on them, saying: "Candice, Crystal, Danielle: The Lord bless you and keep you; the Lord make his face shine upon you and be gracious to you; the Lord turn his face toward you and give you peace. Amen."

You can't imagine the intensity of hugs and beaming faces that come after a prayer like this. Your children won't forget, and neither will you. It's not something to be done casually. At this writing, I've done it only once. But this is what a life of prayer is all about. It's not just words and requests and routine. It's love and power and relationship and heart and soul.

Speak a blessing over your wife or husband too. As I prepare to leave home for work, I occasionally will cup my wife's face in my hands, kiss her gently, and say, "The Lord bless you real good today, sweetheart." Or "The Lord's blessings be all over you from head to toe!" This always evokes a big smile and the tightest squeeze you can imagine. She often blesses me in the same way.

One word of caution: Be sure your life supports whatever your lips speak. Words that are spoken in blessing are invalidated when a child (or spouse) hasn't sensed the daily touch, concern, interest, availability, and care of the blesser. We must take care to build a platform of relationship from which to bless. Remember, the life we lead backs up the words we speak.[2]

7. *Pray through the newspaper.* For those who have trouble coming up with enough things to pray about and for those, who like many people, are addicted to the morning newspaper, this can revolutionize your prayer life.

The paper is full of needs, crises, hurts, and troubles that should cause the heart of the Christian to break. By the time this book makes it into print, the top stories will be different. But these days my newspaper headlines are filled with stories about thirteen smoke jumpers who were killed fighting a wildfire in Colorado; hints from the White House about a possible Haitian invasion (old news by the time this book is in print); abortion protests and a scheduled triple execution in Arkansas; Georgia floods, which have left eighteen people dead and three hundred thousand without safe drinking water and have caused more than $100 million in damages; news from Rwanda that the Tutsis have agreed to a no-fight zone; and more nauseating coverage of the O. J. Simpson hearings. What fertile ground for prayer!

As Adventists with an end-time mind-set, we often look at the news with a prophetic sense of inevitability. "More signs of the times," we say. "Jesus must be coming soon." Sometimes our "sign watching" instills a subtle indifference in our attitudes toward suffering humanity—or, at the very least, a sense of helplessness. But there is something we can do! We can pray.

Each of these stories represents lives, real people who are hurting, desperate, and in need of Jesus. Read the paper with the eyes and heart of Christ, and ask God to mercifully intervene.

With the Hour of Power prayer group at church, I clipped articles from the paper concerning a disturbing rise in youth violence at one of the junior high schools in the community. We prayed that the Holy Spirit would protect the children in our city and bring an end to the violence. In this particular case, the Lord permitted me to be involved in the answer to this prayer.

After initiating a phone call with our city's mayor, I was asked to help draft a letter to the clergy in the area, asking them to rally their congregations in prayer for the well-being of our young people. I was honored to play a part, however small, in being light to the community where God has commanded me to shine.

You may have noticed that the last few action points have touched on intercessory prayer. This one aspect of prayer is so powerful and vital to our experience as Christians that I'm going to deal with it in more detail in the next chapter. (Hang on; it'll blow your socks off!)

So, there you have it. Seven suggestions for putting new passion into your personal prayer journey with God. Not an exhaustive list, by any stretch. You may already be experimenting with several creative forms of prayer that aren't even mentioned here. Great. Go for it. Whatever you do, though, *pray*. Don't just read about it or mentally assent to it. *Pray*. Be real. Be consistent. Be creative. But above all, *pray*. There's so much in store for you if you do.

I'm going to close this chapter with some thoughts from one of my favorite authors and Bible teachers, Charles Swindoll. He ends the third chapter of his book *Flying Closer to the Flame* with an invitation to experience the Holy Spirit in fresh, new ways and adds three thrilling thoughts he asks the reader to ponder. I share them with you now because I think they equally apply to prayer and provide the perfect encouragement for each of us to draw closer to our Father by responding to His call to pray.

So? Move closer. Don't be afraid. Be open and willing to let fresh wonder in. Leave plenty of room for the Spirit to work . . . to move . . . to reveal . . . to bring new dimensions of freedom.

Charles then asks the reader to close his eyes and meditate on three thoughts. For our purposes, I've substituted the word *pray* wherever he used the phrase *fly closer to the flame.*
Imagine that:

- There are realms of earthly experience we have never traveled. (As we [pray], the Spirit can open them up to us.)

Pause and think it over . . .

- There are depths of God's will we have never tapped. (As we [pray], the Spirit can reveal them to us.)

Pause and think it over . . .

- There are dimensions of supernatural power we have never touched. (As we [pray], the Spirit will allow that to happen.)

Pause and think it over . . .[3]

And as you do, receive this blessing from God:

The Lord bless you and keep you;
the Lord make his face shine upon you

and be gracious to you;
the Lord turn his face toward you
and give you peace.
Amen.

---

1. *Closer Than a Brother,* 38, 39.

2. The thoughts expressed in this action point are credited to Pastor Jack Hayford from a taped sermon entitled "The Importance of Blessing Our Children: Passing Our Spiritual Inheritance on to the Next Generation," Gospel Light, Ventura, CA 93006, 1991.

3. Charles R. Swindoll, *Flying Closer to the Flame* (Dallas, Tex.: Word Publishing, 1993), 67, 68.

CHAPTER

11

Much More Passion for Prayer
(Intercession)

I still have the dirt smudges on my shorts and the grime under my fingernails. Even as I type these words, I can still see the dust- and grass-matted hair of the girl and hear the tortured curses of her boyfriend.

Not more than an hour ago, I was eastbound on I-84, returning from the first round of golf I've played in over two months. It had been a gloriously clear and sunny Idaho morning (no resemblance to my game) and, only a couple of miles from my exit, I was beginning to turn my thoughts to an afternoon at the computer with this book. Suddenly, my eye caught movement in the center divider followed by a thick cloud of dust that engulfed the lanes just ahead of me and forced me over onto the shoulder. Someone had rolled his vehicle.

I don't know about you, but I've always wondered about and feared being the first on the scene of an accident. What if people are badly hurt? (I faint at the sight of blood!) What if there are fatalities? Could

I handle it? Would I be able to keep my wits about me? All these thoughts raced through my mind as I, along with several other motorists on the scene, rushed across the highway to help the crash victims.

Two other guys reached the flipped pickup before the rest of us did. As they quickly righted the small truck, I saw the leg of the passenger still inside flop like a rag doll's. My heart was in my throat—I didn't know whether I was seeing the appendage of a badly injured person or a corpse. Whatever, it was too late; I was at the door of the truck.

The driver, a young man, maybe eighteen or nineteen years old, was walking around the battered truck, screaming curses at no one in particular. He was bleeding from some cuts on his arms and legs, and desperation and fear dilated his eyes.

The passenger was a young girl—Molly, she told us. She was alive, thank God, and conscious. Her back was to me and to the other men trying desperately to wrench open the door, but it was no use. The impact had jammed it shut.

One of the helpers sprinted around to the driver's side and, when he couldn't open that door, he slid through the driver's window opening and held onto Molly, assuring her that everything would be OK.

A motorist on the highway above us used his car phone to dial 911, and soon an off-duty EMT scurried down the dusty sides of the recessed median to where we were and gave strict instructions not to move the girl, as she was complaining of head and neck pain.

Once assured that Molly was all right, Jake, the driver, became increasingly agitated, even angry, about trashing his pickup. He continued swearing, and as other helpers were gathering the scattered contents of the pickup, I heard him say, "Those are $400 Rollerblades, and I want them in the truck!" I wondered if he was in shock or just a jerk. Instead of swearing, he should have been thanking God for sparing his life, not to mention being concerned for Molly, who was still trapped, injured, inside the vehicle.

State troopers and paramedics were on the scene in less than ten minutes. They draped a blanket over Molly so she wouldn't get hit with shattering glass; then the Jaws of Life ripped open the jammed door as if it were a pop can. With the professionals there, the rest of us backed out of the way. I felt so helpless standing there—wishing I could do more.

The Holy Spirit must have nudged me right then because I suddenly realized there *was* something more I could do—I could pray. And that's exactly what I did. As the paramedics cut away the crumpled roof and lifted it up and away from the truck's cab, I lifted up in prayer a frightened and injured young woman named Molly, who needed my Father's help.

Right there in the debris-strewn median of I-84, I entered heaven's Oval Office and went boldly before the throne of grace to ask for mercy on behalf of another in her time of need. And I believe the request was granted.

Though I've barely begun to grasp its significance, I believe intercessory prayer to be one of those untouched dimensions of supernatural power that Charles Swindoll was talking about his book in *Flying Closer to the Flame*. Grabbing hold of this one aspect of prayer can redefine your calling and purpose for being a Christian. It has for me.

The purpose and power of intercession

Though it seems at times that our main purpose for being here is to unravel the mystery of the nature of Christ or to decide which forms of worship and music are acceptable or to give in to our insecurities and prejudices and divide conferences along racial lines, our real purpose for being here is to do the works of Jesus and to be channels through which His power to save can flow. Listen to Jesus' own words:

I tell you the truth, anyone who has faith in me will do what I have been doing. He will do even greater things than these, because I am going to the Father. And I will do whatever you ask in my name, so that the Son may bring glory to the Father. You may ask me for anything in my name, and I will do it (John 14:12-14).

Here, Jesus is talking to His disciples about the future of His kingdom and their role in it. Only hours from the cross, He pulls back the curtain of time and allows them to see how they are to operate from now on—and the view is breathtaking!

"Anyone who has faith in me," Jesus says, "will do what I have been doing." What had Jesus been doing? Raising the dead, healing the sick, casting out demons, teaching, blessing, forgiving, loving, and setting people free. When from prison John the Baptist sent his followers to see what Jesus was up to, Jesus sent this word back to John:

"Go back and report to John what you have seen and heard: The blind receive sight, the lame walk, those who have leprosy are cured, the deaf hear, the dead are raised, and the good news is preached to the poor" (Luke 7:22).

This is what Jesus had been doing. And here He says that His disciples—those who have faith in Him—will do the same things. But then He takes it a step farther when He adds, "[They] will do *even greater* things than these." How could this be possible? "Because," Jesus says, "I am going to the Father."

The disciples couldn't appreciate it then, but Jesus' soon return to the Father meant unlimited power was soon to be at their disposal. Proof of this comes in the very next words to fall from Jesus' lips. "And I will do whatever you ask in my name."

Jesus was entrusting His work and kingdom into the hands of His disciples. They were to assume His role and perform even greater works than He did. How? By the power He would possess after He returned to the Father. And "prayer is to be the channel through which that power is received."[1]

Are you getting excited yet? Look at this:

> Their successes and their victories are to be greater than His. Christ mentions two reasons for this. One is that He was going to the Father to receive all power; the other is that they could now ask for and expect that power in His Name. . . . When Jesus was here on earth, He did the greatest works Himself. Devils that the disciples could not cast out fled at His word. When He went to be with the Father, He was no longer here in body to work directly. The disciples were now His Body. All His work from the throne in heaven must and could be done here on earth through them.[2]

If we could only grasp what this means! All His work from the throne in heaven must and can be done here on earth through *you!* Through *me!* Through His army of intercessors who have realized anew their purpose for being Christians in the first place—to give Jesus a body through which He can continue blessing, healing, and redeeming the world!

> To human agencies is committed the work of extending the triumphs of the cross from point to point. . . . To everyone who offers himself to the Lord for service, witholding nothing, is given power for the attainment of measureless results. . . . All that the apostles did, every church member today is to do.[3]

And intercessory *prayer* is the channel through which this power is to be received and distributed.

We are not here merely to sing songs, nod off during the sermon, haggle over religious trivia, complete a tithe envelope, and wait for Jesus to beam us up. We are here to be

> a live wire closing the gap between the saving power of God and the sinful men [and women] who have been cut off from that power. An intercessor is the contacting link between the source of power (the life of the Lord Jesus Christ) and the objects needing that power and life. . . . We are called to be God's transmitters, through whom he can transmit his creative, redemptive, saving power to the minds of other people.[4]

What a purpose! What a privilege! Being religious is such an irrelevant waste of time and energy. But being a conduit of grace—now, there's a worthwhile aspiration—and something this hurting world desperately needs.

When the intercessor needs an intercessor

Ah, but I hear you say that sometimes you're the one who feels cut off from the power—the object needing the life of Jesus. How can you be God's "live wire" when spiritually you feel like such a "dud"?

It's a sad and painful fact that the vital signs of spiritual life in many of our churches indicate that we're near death. The perceived absence of the dynamic presence of the Holy Spirit in either our private or corporate worship experience makes it difficult to find the will or motivation to work for God. We want to save others but so often feel in need of "saving" ourselves. How can we give what we feel we've lost or at least misplaced?

First, realize that Jesus is your intercessor. Hebrews 7:25 assures us that "he is able to save completely those who come to God through him, because he always lives to intercede for them." Twenty-four hours a day, seven days a week, 365 days a year, Jesus is praying for me. There's not a nanosecond of time that elapses when I'm not on His mind. He has called me by His name and has given His life for me. He knows my need. He understands my spiritual dryness, my thirst, my sense of emptiness. And He knows how to water, quench, and fill.

If it feels good to know that another person is praying for you, think about what it means for Jesus to be praying for you! Just thanking Him for His eternal vigilance on your behalf will bring living water to whatever spiritual desert you happen to be going through.

Second, cultivate your own intercessors. Don't stay in a rut and try to go it alone. Ask someone—a trusted friend, a spiritual mentor whom you admire, a spouse or other family member—to be your prayer partner.

When Jesus was feeling cut off from His Father in Gethsemane, He craved the prayer support of His closest friends on earth. He needed their encouragement and strength.

Unfortunately, they were too tired to provide either. (Two thousand years later, things haven't changed much. His disciples are still sleepy!) But that didn't change the fact that He needed to know someone who loved and cared for Him was praying for Him. And if Jesus needed prayer support, can we get along without it?

At the 1990 International Adventist Prayer Conference in Springfield, Oregon, a pastor's wife spoke about her need to cultivate intercessors.

What makes having prayer partners so special is knowing that I have seven women who are anxiously waiting to pray for me. At our prayer partner retreat that I had with these seven women, I opened up to them. I probably shocked some of them, telling them that a pastor's wife's life was not always a bed of roses; how sometimes Sabbath is the worst day of the week for me, especially being a young mother and having small children, and Chad having it be the busiest day of the week. I shared with them how when people want to attack Chad they won't talk to him, they'll talk to me, because they know if they say it to me, then they're really saying it to him. Those of you who are pastors' wives know what I'm talking about. There's a lot of discouragement out there. And for many years I faced it alone. I never talked to women. I never asked anybody to pray for me. But at that retreat with my seven prayer partners, I shared with them specific areas in my life that I wanted them to pray for me, and from that day on I stopped carrying a lot of my burdens by myself.[5]

You may not be a pastor's spouse, but I'm certain discouragement occasionally comes knocking on your door too. If you're serious about victory and about entering into the ministry of intercession, get some intercessors for yourself. Share *specific areas* in your life where you need their prayers, and watch God work.

Third, possess your position as priest and king. Go back and read chapters 4 and 5 if you still struggle with feelings of inadequacy, weakness, and being on the fringes of God's family. We have the highest calling upon our lives—that of being kings and priests for our King Jesus. "You are a chosen people, a *royal priesthood*, a holy nation, a people belonging to God" (1 Peter 2:9, emphasis mine).

A priest may be regarded as one who presents offerings to God, . . . and in this sense every Christian has the privilege of presenting "spiritual sacrifices"—prayer, *intercession*, thanksgiving, glory—to God. . . . Because every Christian is a priest, he may approach God on his own behalf, without the mediation of another human being, and on behalf of others.[6]

At the conclusion of one of our Hour of Power prayer meetings at church, a gentleman I have a great deal of respect for pulled me aside. With tears filling his eyes, he told me of his adult children, who weren't walking with the Lord. "I pray and pray and pray for them every day, but nothing changes. What am I supposed to do?"

How would you like to be asked that question? We had talked before about his children. I knew he loved them and was sincere and faithful in his intercession on their behalf. What should I say? My heart ached for him, and I didn't want to give a glib answer.

I reminded him of Job. Job was a father also. He had seven sons and three daughters. Apparently, they liked to party—heartily and often. If there had been a Robin Leach in Uz, these children of wealth and privilege would surely have been featured on the Mesopotamian version of "Lifestyles of the Rich and Famous."

Whenever these wild parties would finish, Job, acting as the patriarchal priest of his household, would call his children together and "consecrate" them. Then, "early in the morning he would sacrifice a burnt offering for each of them, thinking, 'Perhaps my children have sinned and cursed God in their hearts' " (Job 1:5).

Job's children were living lives of carefree luxury and ease. They were unconcerned about spiritual matters and didn't share their father's devotion to God. Job realized this, and, knowing that his children weren't praying for themselves, he interceded for them and implored divine forgiveness in their behalf.

How many years did Job do this? We don't know. We only know that "this was Job's regular custom" (verse 5). I told my friend that he was to be like Job. That he was the priest of his household and, as such, he could intercede and offer "sacrifice" to God on his children's behalf.

This is what it means to "stand in the gap" for someone else. And, following the example of our great heavenly High Priest, we must persist and keep on praying.

Remember this when praying for those who can't or won't pray for themselves: Our intercession can't force God to save a person against his or her will. God will never violate our freedom of choice. But, like Job, we can ask for mercy, for protection, and for God to keep working on their hearts.

Jesus prayed and wept over Jerusalem, even though its citizens would murder Him in a few short days. He still prayed for their forgiveness and for their souls. As intercessors, we enter into the Lord's sufferings, get out of our self-centered focus, and learn to care for the careless. As we do this, we can be sure that our Father will hear our prayers and won't stop loving, caring for, and reaching out to these "wanderers" as long as breath remains in their bodies and the opportunity to respond exists.

Spiritual vitality will flow into your own walk with Christ as you begin to exercise your authority in prayer and live as "kings and priests" unto God. Andrew Murray writes:

Such men indeed have the power—each in his own area—to obtain and dispense the powers of heaven here on earth. With holy boldness they may make known what they will. . . .

Church of the living God! Your calling is higher and holier than you know! God wants to rule the world through your members. He wants you to be His kings and priests. Your prayers can bestow and withhold the blessings of heaven.[7]

Lastly, bring the water. Our prayer is like pipes, through which water is carried from a large mountain stream to a town some distance away. Such water pipes don't *make* the water willing to flow down from the hills, nor do they give it its power of blessing and refreshment. This is its very nature. All they do is to determine its direction.

In the same way, the very nature of God is to love and to

bless. His love longs to come down to us with its quickening and refreshing streams. But He has left it to prayer to say where the blessing is channeled. He has committed it to His believing people to bring the living water to the desert places.[8]

Not everyone is called to be a missionary. But every Christian is called to be an intercessor. From your living room, you can bring the Living Water of Christ to the desert places in your family, church, community, nation, and world. Go ahead. Intercede for your children, your pastor, your mayor, members of Congress, ADRA relief workers, AIDS victims, gang bangers in this nation's inner cities, the perishing thousands in Rwanda, and for the perishing neighbors you see and associate with every day on your block.

Your Saviour and King waits to cooperate with you in extending the triumphs of His cross and establishing His kingdom. He has gone to the Father to receive ALL power and now wishes to disseminate that power—with greater results—through you and through me. If we will receive and then transmit that resurrection power through intercession, we will not only enjoy much more passion for prayer, but we will also be well on our way to experiencing an ever-deepening passion for the living God.

He guarantees it.

---

1. *With Christ in the School of Prayer*, 140.

2. Ibid., 140, 141.

3. *Testimonies for the Church*, 7:30, 33.

4. Hannah Hurnard, *God's Transmitters* (Wheaton, Ill.: Tyndale House Publishers, Inc., 1978), 18.

5. Taken from the Chad McComas #1 taped session of the International Adventist Prayer Conference, Springfield, Oregon, October 1990, side A. Tapes can be obtained from Oregon Conference Ministerial Department, 13455 S.E. 97th Avenue, Clackamas, OR 97015.

6. Francis D. Nichol, ed., *The Seventh-day Adventist Bible Commentary* (Hagerstown, Md.: Review and Herald Publishing Association, 1980), 7:733.

7. *With Christ in the School of Prayer,* 136.

8. Ibid., 223.

And pray

CHAPTER
12

When Churches Pray
(Corporate Prayer)

Let's play make-believe.

Imagine you're at a prayer meeting that is bursting at the seams with excited people who've come expecting to be changed and to encounter God. Cars line the streets—an overflow from the filled-to-capacity church parking lot. Rooms are bulging with fervent pray-ers. People profess their faith, some are converted or healed, and specific answers to prayer are common and regular.

Got the picture? OK. Now, still imagining this scene, answer this question: Where are you? At your own church's midweek prayer meeting? For some of you reading this, the answer may be Yes. But for most of us, we would really have to be playing make-believe for us to associate this kind of gathering with what regularly goes on in our churches under the name "prayer meeting."

Noting the trend of believers in her day to attend preaching meetings while skipping those for prayer, Ellen White said, "The prayer meetings should be the most interesting gatherings that are held, but these are frequently poorly managed."[1]

Indeed, many churches today have even discontinued weekly prayer meetings. Peter Wagner observes, "Many that still have them admit the meetings have become routine, dull and lifeless, generating little action prayer either for the church or for the community."[2]

Why is the prayer meeting often the loneliest and most poorly attended event of the week? What has happened to our corporate prayer experience that has sapped it of its vital power and place in our lives?

Any book calling God's people to prayer and revival in the waning hours of earth's history would be incomplete without addressing the purpose, privilege, and need for corporate prayer. Personal prayer, as important as it is in our walk with Christ, is only one facet of God's divine directive to "humble ourselves and pray." Corporate (or group) prayer is equally important and must be restored to a place of prominence in the life of the church.

Why corporate prayer?

You may be wondering, If a person enjoys a rich and satisfying personal prayer life at home, why is praying in a group even necessary? Groups may not be your "thing." Besides, the prayer meetings that you are accustomed to may have all the excitement of a field trip to your local Laundromat laundry! Why leave the comfort of your home after a hard day's work to be bored stiff in a poorly ventilated room, listening to long prayers for requests that seem to remain on the list for years with no apparent answers?

Why indeed? Corporate prayer was never meant to be this way. Scripture gives us a dynamic picture of the role prayer played in Christ's newly established church.

As soon as the disciples returned to Jerusalem following Jesus' ascension, they gathered for prayer (Acts 1:12-14). On the Day of

Pentecost, they were all together in one place, praying for the promised blessing of the Holy Spirit, when the church was born and three thousand new believers were added to the group (Acts 2:1, 41). Prayer was one of primary activities of their church life (Acts 2:42), and the apostles considered prayer to be their primary duty (Acts 6:4).

The book of Acts is replete with examples of the young church at prayer: for Peter's release from prison (12:5), to appoint new elders (14:23), and when calling the first missionaries (13:3).

"Corporate prayer," as Peter Wagner says, "was not peripheral back then as it often is now. It was central."[3] And many times when those believers united their voices together in prayer, "the place where they were meeting was shaken. And they were all filled with the Holy Spirit and spoke the word of God boldly" (Acts 4:31). No snooze sessions, these!

But why is this experience still necessary now? For the same reasons it was essential then. Release of power, unity, fellowship, and encouragement.

Release of power

The early Church visibly depended on prayer as the means of releasing the power of God. Their belief in the role of public prayer was clear: "If we do not pray, God will not act." They understood there existed a hope and a unique spiritual power in the prayers of the Church that did not exist in their experiences of private prayer.[4]

If only we believed that today! Don't we want to see the power of God released in our lives? In the lives of our unsaved loved ones? In the church? The public-school system? The jails and rehab centers? The refugee camps in Tanzania?

Whoa! Hold everything. Maybe these questions should be more

than rhetorical. Perhaps we've stumbled upon one of the major reasons corporate prayer languishes in so many of our churches. Perhaps a release of God's power is not high on our list of priorities.

Think about it.

Why seek God for power? The need for power indicates an intention or desire to *do something*. It pains me to say it, but the truth is, we're content to do *nothing*.

Oh, sure, we're willing to perpetuate the machinery. We'll accept a church office once in a while, and we'll sacrifice our sleep occasionally to make it to church and do our Christian "duty"—but you don't need divine power to do that. Hey, we can do the "church thing" with our eyes closed. It's easy and doesn't require much effort.

The early church was on fire with the mission of saving souls. Are we?

> The disciples felt their spiritual need and cried to the Lord for the holy unction that was to fit them for the work of soul saving. They did not ask for a blessing for themselves merely. They were weighted with the burden of the salvation of souls. They realized that the gospel was to be carried to the world, and they claimed the power that Christ had promised.[5]

And maybe this is at least one reason why our prayer meetings are so dry and lifeless. We're not seeking God for the desire and power to do what we're here to do—share the gospel. And if this isn't a goal we're willing to pursue, then perhaps the prayer meeting is better off being discontinued. It may be well on its way to being an empty form. A ritual. A tradition that has long since lost its meaning and purpose.

If we don't have a heart for the lost or an inclination to work for souls, let this be our first confession and request in the prayer meeting. Then let's seek the release of God's power that will enable us to do this work.

Unity

Jesus said, "Again, I tell you that if two of you on earth agree about anything you ask for, it will be done for you by my Father in heaven. For where two or three come together in my name, there am I with them" (Matthew 18:19, 20).

Corporate prayer provides an opportunity for the body of Christ to experience the power of agreement. Individual prayer is great and is the lifeblood of the believer, but here Jesus is letting us know that something special happens when children of His agree in prayer.

Actually, it really *is* something special when God's children agree on anything! Disagreeing on everything from which version of the Bible is best to the appropriateness of drama in the worship service is in vogue. It seems as if everything is open to interpretation, and consensus is as endangered as the spotted owl.

When Quincy Jones, the famous record producer, assembled the all-star recording cast for the "We Are the World" project, he hung a sign outside the recording studio that read: "Check your egos at the door." He knew that the singers he was working with were superstars with temperaments, styles, and attitudes as different and individual as the colors on a peacock. Yet if they were to succeed, they would have to surrender that individuality and "symphonize" together to create a unified sound.

And so it is with group prayer, where the differing wills and ideas of two or more believers must symphonize as one sound to God. . . .

When two or more believers come together to pray, they often come with different ideas about what to ask and a different understanding about what the will of God is in the matter. One may think that God wants to heal the sick. Another may think that He is bringing a trial of illness to teach the afflicted. But as they seek agreement and unity of request, they begin to hear the voice of God gradually conforming their differing thoughts or "reasoning" (1 Tim. 2:8) into the will of God. And their prayer is answered.[6]

Fellowship and encouragement

We need each other! Like the pastor's wife I quoted in the previous chapter says, there's a lot of discouragement out there. We need to hold the hand of our brothers and sisters and let them know we care. We need to see that we're not alone in our struggles. Others, just like us, carry the same burdens and stub their toes on some of the same sharp edges of life that we do.

How to breathe new life into the corporate prayer meeting

Even a prayer meeting in full cardiac arrest can be helped by trying the following suggestions.

1. *Pray with music.* "Music can be a great power for good, yet we do not make the most of this branch of worship."[7] Our people need to be taught that singing is a form of prayer and not "filler" or the warm-up. Give the first ten minutes of the meeting to singing the prayers. Use worship songs that address God directly, and learn to sing unto the Lord with gladness.

2. *Keep it simple.* Again, we need to educate the church on how to pray in a group. Home is the place for longer, more personal prayer. Those who skip secret prayer at home and try to make up for it with long prayers at the corporate meeting are "conference and prayer meeting killers,"[8] according to Ellen White. "All should feel it a Christian duty to pray short. Tell the Lord just what you want, without going all over the world."[9]

Praying "conversationally" is a method we've used at the Hour of Power gatherings with great success. Praying in this fashion gives you opportunity to pray several times but addresses only one subject at a time. This also promotes agreement among the petitioners. When one person asks for God to bring reconciliation to a troubled marriage, another in the group can pick up the conversation and "agree" with that person's request by saying something like: "And, Father, I agree with Janice right now and ask You to bring a spirit of forgiveness into the hearts of this young couple."

3. *Cut the prayer list down to size.* "Long prayer lists are the sign of a healthy congregation, but they are also the killers of corporate prayer. Identify a few of the most critical, widespread concerns for the focus of your group prayer time. Then ask smaller prayer groups or individuals to take the rest of the concerns to God in prayer."[10]

4. *Be specific.* Vague, general prayers should be "edited" by the group until a specific need is identified. Charles Mackintosh writes:

> The simple fact is, we are too vague and, as a consequence, too indifferent in our prayers and prayer-meetings. We do not seem like people asking for what they want, and waiting for what they ask. This is what destroys our prayer-meetings, rendering them pithless, pointless, powerless; turning them into teaching or talking-meetings, rather than deep-toned, earnest prayer meetings.[11]

5. *Share answers to prayer.* "In church after church," says Peter Wagner,

> I have seen prayer lists published by the church office, some of them elaborate. But in fewer than 1 out of 10 have I seen regular reports of the *answers* to these prayers. Prayer may change history, but the people who do it won't get excited about it if they do not know it is happening.[12]

135

In my own church, we publish a "prayer alert" column in our bulletin with names of individuals the church is praying for. Unfortunately, we don't have a "prayer response" column reporting the results of those prayers. We must find ways to do this in every corporate prayer meeting.

6. *Change the name.* This may seem silly, but among the people I work with, if the word *meeting* is mentioned, folks start checking their watches and digging for their car keys. Let's face it, we're meetinged-out. Change a negative association into a positive one by renaming your corporate prayer time something like the "prayer gathering" or "praise gathering." Or come up with something completely radical like "Hour of Power."

7. *Call the church together for special seasons of prayer.* In other words, don't let the midweek service be the only time for corporate prayer. Let the church come together on the National Day of Prayer, during the Christmas season, on Good Friday, in preparation for evangelistic meetings, at the beginning of the year, and at special times of seeking spiritual renewal. The special thirty-day prayer season mentioned in chapter 2 is a good example of this.

This list could certainly be expanded, but use it as a jumping-off place for jump-starting your corporate prayer meetings.

The prayer ministry in your church

How important is prayer in the overall life and functioning of the church? Consider what Ellen White saw in vision concerning this:

I saw that a thick cloud enveloped them, but that a few rays of light from Jesus pierced this cloud. I looked to see those who received this light, and saw individuals earnestly praying for victory. . . . The light of heaven was shed upon them; but the cloud of darkness over the church in general was thick. They were stupid and sluggish. . . .

Satan has come down in great power, knowing that his time is short. His angels are busy, and a great share of the people of God suffer themselves to be lulled to sleep by him. The cloud again passed over, and settled upon the church. I saw that it would be only by earnest effort and persevering prayer that this spell would be broken.[13]

Now. I'll ask again. How important is prayer in the life of your church?

The other day, and I randomly selected several churches to call and conduct a brief survey. When someone answered, usually the church secretary, I would introduce myself and my project and ask if they would answer a few questions about their prayer ministries.

The questions were: (1) Does your church have an organized congregational prayer ministry led by a prayer leader (staff position or lay leadership position)? (2) Does your church have a prayer room or designated prayer center? (3) Does your church have prayer chains? (4) Based on the prayer activities/programs in your church, would you say that prayer is a high priority?

Though admittedly unscientific, the responses were nevertheless enlightening. I phoned an Assembly of God church, two Baptist churches, a nondenominational church, an Apostolic church, and a Seventh-day Adventist church. Only one of the churches answered Yes to three out of the four questions. While most expressed a wish to see more happen in their churches to promote prayer, the current interest and commitment for most was "average" at best.

How is it where you worship? What would it take to heighten the interest for an ongoing, organized prayer ministry in your pastor, elders, or willing fellow members?

The corporate prayer life of the body of Christ should not be left to happenstance or to shrivel up like a raisin in the sun. If we're ever to break through the Laodicean cloud that hangs so thickly over us, our churches are going to have to become praying churches. Churches where the Sword of the Spirit is wielded with the Holy Spirit–sharpened energy of prayer.

Time is running out. We've played make-believe long enough. Our churches must become *real* centers of earnest prayer now, before Jesus and the world who needs us pronounce our game over.

Author's note

If you would like more ideas on how to make yours a praying church, I'd recommend the following resources:

1. Alvin J. Vander Griend with Edith L. Bajema, *The Praying Church Sourcebook* (Church Development Resources, 2850 Kalamazoo Ave., SE, Grand Rapids, MI 49560, copyright 1990).

2. C. Peter Wagner, *Churches That Pray*.

While I can't endorse everything in these books, there are plenty of solid ideas that will prove a real blessing.

---

1. *Testimonies for the Church,* 4:70.

2. *Churches That Pray,* 106.

3. Ibid., 107.

4. Kent R. Wilson, "The Lost Art of Group Prayer," *Discipleship Journal* (March/April 1994), 44.

5. Ellen G. White, *The Acts of the Apostles* (Boise, Idaho: Pacific Press Publishing Association, 1911), 37.

6. "The Lost Art of Group Prayer," *Discipleship Journal,* 44.

7. *Testimonies for the Church,* 4:71.

8. Ibid., 2:578.

9. Ibid.

10. Kent R. Wilson, "Ten Ways to Put Life Back Into Group Prayer," *Discipleship Journal* (March/April 1994), 45.

11. Quoted in "The Lost Art of Group Prayer," *Discipleship Journal,* 47

12. *Churches That Pray,* 122.

13. *Testimonies for the Church,* 1:178.

Part 6

And seek my face

"You will seek me and find me when you seek me with all your heart."
—*Jeremiah 29:13*

"Until our passion for finding God is deeper than any other passion, we will arrange life according to our taste, not God's."
—*Dr. Larry Crabb*

Real prayer happens when our desire to submit to God's power outweighs our desire to harness it.

C H A P T E R
13

For God and God Alone

"There is none that calleth upon thy name, that stirreth up himself to take hold of thee" (Isaiah 64:7, KJV).

I wonder if this text was on the mind of the pastor who sat at a friend's dining-room table and confessed his frustration over an inability to motivate his members to commit themselves to something other than their own convenience. The stoop of his shoulders suggested weariness and discouragement. "It's hard to think about vision," he said dejectedly, "when attendance is still the main problem."

Is this an isolated case? A problem unique to this one disheartened pastor who was beginning to question his ability to minister effectively? I think not.

I don't know when it happened, but slowly, almost imperceptibly, the biblical Christianity that we see demonstrated in the early church has given way to something quite different in today's church. If Paul or Barnabas or Steven or Priscilla were resurrected and allowed to visit our churches, would they be able to tell that we follow the same Master? That we've pledged our allegiance to the same cause? That we claim citizenship in the same kingdom?

More and more, it seems that the gospel of Christ has been replaced by the gospel of convenience, in which the highest goal in our religious exercises is the achievement of our own personal comfort. We often seek God's power more to relieve our pain, improve our self-esteem, heal our past hurts, and clear the way for our enjoyment of an affluent, trouble-free life than to make us like Jesus.

Dr. Larry Crabb describes the current crisis in Christianity perfectly when he writes:

> We Christians cannot talk about loving God until we come to grips with our raging passion for ourselves. We can not and will not love anyone but ourselves until we meet God in a way that stirs us to race after him with single-minded intensity, until our deepest desire is to get to know him better.
>
> And that's our problem. In a culture so thoroughly devoted to life now, and in a church drenched with teaching on self-improvement and building happier lives, we can't easily develop a passion for something other than our immediate satisfaction. The historic church, in its role as embassy of a foreign kingdom, taught that the chief end of people is to glorify God and enjoy him forever; the modern church too often teaches that the chief end of God is to gratify people.[1]

The multitude that Jesus fed with the loaves and fishes had their priorities mixed up too. Desperate to make Jesus king so He could chase the Romans from Palestine and make their lives easier, they scrambled into their fishing boats and tracked the Master down in Capernaum.

Jesus knew the real reason they were looking for Him. They wanted more miracles, full bellies, and a leader who would make them great. Jesus read this in their hearts and said, "Truly, truly, I say to you, you seek Me, not because you saw signs, but because you ate of the loaves, and were filled" (John 6:26, NASB).

Today, it's not loaves and fishes we demand, but freedom from all problems and the independence to pursue our own happiness. When it comes to church, we demand good teaching, the best music, the finest children's divisions, and the best preaching (provided, of course, it's thirty minutes or less and finished by noon!). Obviously, there is nothing wrong with having well-trained musicians and an excellent choir. Of course, our children should have the best we can give them. And our pastors should strive to bring their congregations the best food the Word of God provides. But we are often carried away by the trappings of worship, the enhancements to praise, while missing the *object* of that worship and praise, Christ Himself.

And who wants problems? I want a happy, successful life as much as anyone else. But if this is all we're about—if our pursuit of God has only these objectives in view—then Christ has every right to turn to us as He did to Andrew and John when they first followed Him and ask, "What do you seek?" (John 1:38, NASB).

What do we seek? What is our chief end as Seventh-day Adventist Christians living in the eleventh hour of earth's history? Does our passion for God and His glory outweigh our passion for early retirement, a new home or car, career advancement, leisure, getting married, or educational pursuits? Are we here to serve God, or is He "a waiter who, at the snap of our fingers, runs out of heaven's kitchen loaded down with trays of food to fill our empty stomachs"[2]? Why are you a Christian? Why follow Jesus? And are we really following Him? Is there anyone left who calls upon God's name and stirs himself up to take hold of Him?

The third directive

The answer, of course, is Yes. God still has a people. Weak? Yes. Unreliable? Yes. Self-centered and willful? Yes. But they are still His, called by His name. And it is these whom God addresses in the third directive of our key text. *"If my people, who are called by my name will [1] humble themselves [2] and pray [3] AND SEEK MY FACE . . ."*

What does it mean to seek God's face? I believe it simply means to pursue God Himself above all else. To let His purposes, His priorities, and His agenda matter most in our lives.

This seeking of God's "face" does not have to be left on the theoretical plane. It can be a matter of practical reality. Take, for example, the company whose management team seek God's face in running their business and wait for His answer before acting.

From the very beginning we have followed a simple pattern: we usually discuss our problems the day before, then we sleep on them. The next morning we start our day in prayer, offering up these problems to God. Each day leadership rotates to a different member of the team who opens by reading a chapter from the New Testament. Next this leader may pray extemporaneously and then he leads us in the Lord's Prayer.

In the period of silence we then offer up ourselves and our problems to God and *listen* for His answers. We always write down any thoughts and directions that come to us, and toward the end of our time together the leader asks each one to read whatever he has written. If a specific problem is not answered, or if we are in disagreement about it, we never act on it. We offer it up during the day in individual prayer and at the next meeting, until God's answer becomes clear. I do not order my executives to do anything. We either act in love and unison, or not at all. Each meeting concludes with intercessory prayers for anyone who requests them.[3]

For God and God Alone

I know that some readers would say that this practice borders on the fanatical. That attempting to operate a business or a church like this is unrealistic, naive, and could never happen in the "real world." Why? Because too many egos need stroking, and too many political agendas need juggling. To this, I say, *Amen!* There are altogether too much ego and politics in what we do "for God" and not nearly enough of the Holy Spirit's leading.

Power shortage

In the December 1991 issue of *Ministry*, J. H. Zachary, associate secretary of the Ministerial Association at the General Conference, recounts being stunned by a statement made by the Southern Asia Division president. "Of all the work the church has accomplished," the president began, "95 percent of it could have been done without the aid of the Holy Spirit."

Could this be true? Could great institutions, powerful evangelism programs, and mighty mission strategies be developed without the Spirit? Without the seeking of God's face?

Andrew Murray, the great missionary to South Africa, knew that this scenario was very possible and, indeed, the reality in most of Christendom when he wrote:

I may preach or write or think or meditate, and delight in being occupied with things in God's Book and in God's Kingdom; and yet the power of the Holy Ghost may be markedly absent. I fear that if you take the preaching throughout the Church of Christ and ask why there is, alas! so little converting power in the preaching of the Word, why there is so much work and often so little result for eternity, why the Word has so little power to build up believers in holiness and in consecration— the answer will come: It is the absence of the power of the Holy Ghost. And why is this? There can be no other reason but that the flesh and human energy have taken the place that the Holy Ghost ought to have.[4]

The flesh and human energy! God has given each of us certain talents and abilities. Some of us are charismatic personalities who find it easy to be up front and lead out in various programs of the church. Others of us are creative and have the ability to sing, paint, write, or play an instrument in a way that moves people. Praise the Lord for these blessings!

But we must recognize and avoid a subtle trap that most Christians are unaware of. *If we use these gifts in our own strength, we will have a measure of success.* And how deceptive that success can be! It can, in fact, blind us to the real thing and keep us satisfied with mere trickles, when God is willing to send great showers of blessing. By force of character or talent, we can accomplish something for God. But not nearly what *could* be accomplished if we sought God's face for the defeat of self and for complete submission to the power and will of the Holy Spirit.

And this we must do *first. Before* the plans are laid and the blueprints are drawn. Remember this: *Human wisdom empties the cross of Christ of its power* (see 1 Corinthians 1:17; 2:1, 4, 5)! If we're not careful, faith can be swallowed up in formulas. Prayer can become a "rubber stamp" on proposals and projects that bear our insignia, not God's.

"Prayer is usually the last thing I *naturally* tend to do," says author William Carr Peel.

I can study about prayer and talk about it, but actually praying is something else. I am a doer; I find it very natural to jump into something up to my eyeballs. I tend to plan first and then *baptize my strategies with a little prayer* to soothe my conscience. I often exhaust my own strength before turning to the spiritual resources at my disposal as a child of God. It makes me wonder at times what might have been had I stopped to talk things over with God first.[5]

It's time to seek the Lord

As I said in the first chapter of this book, it's time to pray. We've worked in our own strength and worshiped according to our convenience for so long we've forgotten what the moving of the Holy Spirit on our hearts feels like. Indicators throughout the church—declining tithe, declining membership, the absence of Baby Boomers, Valugenesis reports, etc.—tell us that something has got to change. And that "something" is the halfhearted way we now seek God's face for the release of the Holy Spirit.

If it is our faith that God is going to have mercy on His Church in these last ages, it will be because the doctrine and the truth about the Holy Spirit will not only be studied, but sought after with a whole heart; and not only because that truth will be sought after, but because ministers and congregations will be found bowing before God in deep abasement with one cry: "We have grieved God's Spirit; we have tried to be Christian churches with as little as possible of God's Spirit; we have not sought to be churches filled with the Holy Ghost."

All the feebleness in the Church is owing to the refusal of the Church to obey its God.[6]

Charles Spurgeon also testified to the importance of the Holy Spirit's reign in the church by saying:

If we do not have the Spirit of God, it were better to shut up the churches, to nail up the doors, to put a black cross on them and say, "God have mercy on us." If your ministers have not the

Spirit of God you had better not preach, and your people had better stay at home. I think I speak not too strongly when I say that a church in the land without the Spirit of God is rather a curse than a blessing.

And what about the indicators in our own lives? The schedule that is too busy for prayer? The Bible that goes unread for weeks or months at a time? A missing joy in worship or the absence of the sweet sense of God's presence as we work and play? Are we, like the hungry multitude in Capernaum, passionately pursuing the "meat that perisheth" more than the "meat which endureth unto everlasting life"?

I know that sounds very religious. I don't mean it to. The bottom line is that we can't go on like this any longer. We must "seek the Lord while he may be found; [and] call on him while he is near" (Isaiah 55:6).

And how are we to seek and call on the Lord? Greater efforts to obey? Less television? More sacrificial giving? Joining a cell group? Consistent "quiet times"? A longer prayer list? Being at church every time the doors are open? Reading the Bible all the way through? C'mon. We've attempted all these things before, right? And for a time, we felt spiritually renewed and as if we were finally seeking God with all our hearts. But it doesn't last, does it? A list of good works won't bring God any closer; only faith in His promise to be found will.

Seeking God

So how do we do it? Begin by praying for a heart that follows hard after God. Put another way, ask to fall in love with Jesus. I can't look into your heart, and you can't look into mine. We may be following Jesus very dutifully, but with no real love for Him. If the passion has gone out of your relationship with Christ, ask Him to rekindle it. Ask Him to make you thirst—not for power to work in the church—

but for power to love Him more than you love yourself.

Next, ask God to help you realize that time spent with Him is life to you. This cannot be optional for the Christian who is seeking God's face. "Love the Lord your God, listen to his voice, and hold fast to him. *For the Lord is your life*" (Deuteronomy 30:20, emphasis mine).

Time with God to read His Word and fellowship with Him must become more valuable to us than our "necessary food" (see Job 23:12). It may not be this way for you now, but ask for it, and believe that He will answer your prayer.

It was A. W. Tozer who said, "The secret of successful Christians has been that they had a sweet madness for Jesus about them." Those who seek God's face will have a sweet madness for Jesus about them. His will, His glory, His kingdom, and He Himself will become their hearts' desire. And when this happens, one result is certain: the Holy Spirit will be returned to His rightful place of honor in our homes, churches, and lives—and revival will come!

A song and a prayer

I wanted to end this chapter with a story. A powerful illustration that would somehow sum up the heart of what it means to seek God's face. I didn't have one.

But I do have a prayer song that I want to leave you with. If you know it, please include it in your prayers every day as you seek to know and love the Lord with all your heart. If you don't, ask for it at your local Adventist Book Center or Christian bookstore. Learn the simple tune, and let it express the deepest longing of your soul for the One who calls you by name.

As the Deer
As the deer panteth for the water,
so my soul longeth after Thee.

IF MY PEOPLE PRAY

You alone are my heart's desire,
and I long to worship Thee.
You alone are my strength, my shield;
To You alone may my spirit yield.
You alone are my heart's desire,
and I long to worship Thee.[7]

---

1. Larry Crabb, *Finding God* (Grand Rapids, Mich.: Zondervan Publishing House, 1993), 46.

2. Ibid., 19.

3. William Carr Peel, *What God Does When Men Pray* (Colorado Springs, Colo.: NavPress, 1933), 39, 40.

4. Andrew Murray, *Absolute Surrender* (Chicago, Ill.: Moody Press), 87.

5. *What God Does When Men Pray,* 52.

6. *Absolute Surrender,* 89, 90.

7. Words and music by Martin Nystrom. Copyright 1984 Maranatha! Music (Administered by The Copyright Company, Nashville, TN) / ASCAP. All Rights Reserved. International Copyright Secured. Used by Permission.

CHAPTER
14

Send Revival!

A geranium basket hangs on my front porch. Only moments ago, I stood at my office window and saw a hummingbird sipping nectar from the pink blossoms. I watched in amazement as the tiny bird, in a blur of wings, darted from flower to flower, inserting its beak into the centers to extract sweet refreshment.

Never having seen a hummingbird around our place before, I was eager to have someone else watch with me. I eventually got my daughter Candice to join me at the window. It was fun for both of us. Then, as quickly as it had come, the thirsty bird flew away. So what's the big deal? How did this insignificant incident merit mention here in this book? Stay with me.

Only a few days ago, I came very close to throwing out that geranium. It's been a very hot July in Idaho this summer. Temperatures have hovered right at or just below the century mark for more than two weeks. All the plants at the front of the house have been withering under the intense heat of the Idaho sun. My geranium plant is no exception. It, too, was dying.

The leaves were curling and turning lunch-sack brown. The pink blossoms were shrinking into tight whitish knots, and the soil felt like a hardened sponge to the touch. I thought it was a goner. Nevertheless, I took the plant down and gave it a good soaking in the backyard. I later returned the plant to its hook over the front porch. But as the days went by and it didn't seem to be recovering, I was ready to toss it and buy another one.

The hummingbird's visit this morning, however, helped me to see something I had missed. The geranium wasn't dead. True, it still had brown leaves on it, and there were still shriveled blossoms, but I hadn't noticed all the new growth that had taken place since I last watered it. There were buds on that geranium plant that I never thought would open. But when the cool water soaked into the parched soil, new life surged through those thirsty roots and burst open the buds I'd given up for dead. *My geranium experienced revival,* and a passing hummingbird found refreshment in its flowers.

And here is the point. Despite appearances, the church isn't dead yet, either. There is still life in its members. But there are times when it sure looks like a goner.

There have been times I've sat in Adventist worship services and had to fight the urge to check pulses. I distinctly remember walking into one service thinking I'd come in during a special-music number. The two women up front singing a duet out of the hymnal sounded lovely. But it wasn't until they stopped to announce the next hymn that I realized they were leading a song service!

The people around me had songbooks in their hands, and their lips were moving, but no sound was coming out! According to their song, they served "a risen Saviour"; but from the way they were singing, you'd have thought they were at His funeral.

On the other end of the spectrum are the "live" churches. The ones with fiery preaching, good music, and responsive audiences who aren't afraid to clap, shout, raise their hands, and show emotion in their worship of God. But as I used to hear the preachers say when I was growing up, "It's not how high you jump on Sabbath, but how straight you walk when you come down."

The presence of emotion in the "live" church isn't an iron-clad guarantee that the Spirit is being honored in greater measure there than at the "dead" church. After all the shouting's done, the jealousy, backstabbing, and pride are often as much on display later that week as were the tears on Sabbath. In some cases, emotionalism is a cover for the missing authentic presence of God.

It's like what happened to a well-known, well-loved gospel recording artist who was found weeping offstage just before a big concert. Friends, obviously concerned, hovered around and attempted to comfort him. "What's the matter? What's troubling you?" they asked.

Between sobs, the broken singer replied, "I don't know when it happened, but I've lost the anointing. I've lost the sense of God's presence." As shocked as his friends were to hear this admission, imagine their surprise when the man, scrambling to recover from his display of vulnerability, collected himself and said, "But that's OK. I can make it on what I have left."

Too many Christians—electrified and petrified—are trying to make it on what they have left.

Through busyness, compromise, and neglect, we've allowed our relationship with God to become habitual, cordial, and bland. Like a marriage with no intimacy, we've become roommates instead of lovers. The arrangement is convenient but boring.

The letters-to-the-editor pages of our Adventist journals often reflect a loss of vision, and they mirror the truth of John Sein's statement, "In the absence of a great dream, pettiness prevails."

Our attendance at Amway rallies is sometimes more regular than our attendance at church, and if our young people remain missing from our churches much longer, we may have to start putting their faces on the sides of milk cartons.

Signs of dehydration are prevalent. Our souls are parched. Our gullets are painful and hard. We're dry and desperate for the refreshing waters of the Holy Spirit. Yet many of us have become so accustomed to the Spirit's absence that, like various desert plants, we've adapted to our dry habitat.

Desert dwellers

Some desert plants have spreading, shallow roots that are able to quickly take up surface moisture from heavy dews and occasional rains. Similarly, when we adapt to spiritual dryness, we become shallow Christians who are "too easily satisfied with a ripple on the surface, when it is our privilege to expect the deep moving of the Spirit of God."[1]

Because we take in so little of God's Word and spend so few moments with Him in prayer, our Christian experience doesn't run very deep. We're easily offended, easily discouraged, easily bored with the things of God. We're spiritual babes, "capable of nothing much more than nursing at the breast" (1 Corinthians 3:2, The Message).

Desert plants have other ways of adapting to drought. Some plants, called succulents, store water in thick, fleshy tissue of leaves, stems, and roots. Thorns, which are modified leaves, serve to guard the water from animal invaders. For desert-adapted Christians, when there's not much of the Holy Spirit around, the little we get is hoarded. We don't have enough of our own to share with someone else, so we guard what we have, becoming tight, pinched, and thorny. This could very well explain some of the pained expressions sadly common on the faces of many churchgoers. Sitting on thorns hurts!

But let's not be too hasty to throw the church away.

Send Revival!

Down but not out

"A man had a fig tree," Jesus told a crowd one day:

> planted in his vineyard, and he went to look for fruit on it, but did not find any. So he said to the man who took care of the vineyard, "For three years now I've been coming to look for fruit on this fig tree and haven't found any. Cut it down! Why should it use up the soil?"
>
> "Sir," the man replied, "leave it alone for one more year, and I'll dig around it and fertilize it. If it bears fruit next year, fine! If not, then cut it down" (Luke 13:6-8).

Despite our shriveled blossoms and stunted growth, the Lord has no intentions of tossing us out. However prevalent the signs of death and dryness, the church, like my geranium, is still alive, and the Lord Himself will tend to it (see Isaiah 27:2, 3). I agree with my friend Clifford Goldstein when he says, "No matter how bad the church supposedly is, the Lord is still using it—and it alone—to bring this special message to the world."[2]

Yes, the church is still alive. But it desperately needs revival!

What water and fertilizer are to the nutrient-poor, thirsty soil, revival is to the Spirit-poor, thirsty members of God's church. If we as a people humble ourselves, pray, and earnestly seek God's face for revival, will it come? Can our prayers bring revival?

Revival praying

The answer is obviously Yes. The very text this entire book is about contains God's promise to send revival in response to the earnest prayers of His people. "If my people, who are called by my name, will humble themselves and pray and seek my face and turn from their wicked ways, *then will I hear from heaven and will forgive their sin and will heal their land.*"

The forgiveness of our sins and the healing of our churches from Laodiceanism will come when we pray. Ellen White said, "A revival need be expected only in answer to prayer."[3] And Dr. A. T. Pierson concluded, "There has never been a spiritual awakening in any country or locality that did not begin in united prayer."

Such was the case in 1857, when a church janitor named Jeremiah Lamphier instigated a spiritual awakening in this country with a simple invitation to prayer.

Six people showed up the first week, fourteen the next, and twenty-three the next. They decided to meet every day. Soon filling their first location, they spilled over to the Methodist church, and then to every public building in downtown New York. Horace Greeley's reporter could get around to only twelve meetings during the noon hour, but counted *6,100 men—praying men!*[4]

This revival swept New England. Ten thousand a week were being converted in New York alone. Prayer meetings in the churches were held at 8:00 in the morning, 12:00 noon, and again at 6:00 in the evening. Revealing the scope and impact of this revival, Dr. J. Edwin Orr, one of this country's foremost authorities on the subject of spiritual awakenings, said, "The Baptists had so many people to baptize they couldn't fit them in their churches."

Millions of people came to know Christ during the four decades following this revival. And it all started because someone decided to pray!

The Welsh revival of 1904; the Second Great Awakening in the second quarter of the nineteenth century, which gave rise to Adventism; the Reformation; and even the birth of the church itself on the Day of Pentecost—all these movements began with prayer.

It's no different today. Our prayers for revival can and will make a difference. God promises that. But before we can see the evidences of spiritual life surging anew through the church and in our world, there are at least six things we must consider as we take up the work of seeking God's face for revival. Let's prayerfully look at each of these.

We must be willing to be revived. The only thing preventing revival from coming is the lack of interest on the part of God's people in pursuing it. This may seem harsh, but it's present truth. "There must be earnest effort to obtain the blessing of the Lord, not because God is not willing to bestow His blessing upon us, but *because we are unprepared to receive it.*"[5]

If revival were something we wanted, we'd have it, because Jesus is more willing to give the Holy Spirit than we are to receive it. There is no supply failure in God. No power shortage on His end. Why would He withhold the one gift from His church that "brings all other gifts in its train"? Why hold back what His children need most? Because His children haven't asked. They haven't wanted the gift as badly as He's wanted to give it.

Why? *Because we're comfortable with things just the way they are!* Spiritually speaking, we're not too hot, not too cold. We're just right. Frankly, lukewarm suits us.

But more and more of God's people are growing weary of the status quo. They're coming together in small groups and meeting early in the morning for prayer and attending conferences on the Holy Spirit in an attempt to break free from the tepid malaise that keeps us in spiritual diapers. They realize that the focus of their prayers must first be on themselves.

"We must enter upon the work individually."[6]

On those who believe that a revival is needed and is possible rests the solemn responsibility of preparing the way of the Lord in speaking to God and men and women about it. To God we speak about it in prayer. We ask Him to *open our own eyes and hearts,* and those of our church, to what He thinks and says of the spiritual life He finds. *We confess our own sin* and the sin of our brethren. We give *ourselves* to stand in the gap, to take hold of God's strength.[7]

Before I seek God for the revival of the many, I must seek Him for the revival of one—me.

Praying for revival takes work. Anything worth having is worth working for. If I heard my parents tell me that once when I was growing up, I heard it a thousand times. But it's so true. Things that matter, the important things, the things that bring us long-term satisfaction and rewards, these usually require some sweat. Colleges don't have degree giveaways, financial independence isn't obtained from the sofa, and good marriages don't just "happen." They require commitment, perseverance, and work.

Do we think that the resuscitation of God's church from near spiritual death can be accomplished without effort? If so, we need to think again. Satan has worked long and hard to keep Christians in a spiritual coma, and the spell isn't easily broken.

The great controversy between Christ and Satan, that has been carried forward for nearly six thousand years, is soon to close; and the wicked one *redoubles* his efforts to defeat the work of Christ in man's behalf and to fasten souls in his snares. . . .

When there is no special effort made to resist his power, when indifference prevails in the church and the world, Satan is not concerned; for he is in no danger of losing those whom he is leading captive at his will. . . .

Satan well knows that all whom he can lead to neglect prayer and the searching of the Scriptures, will be overcome by his attacks. Therefore he invents every possible device to engross the mind.[8]

The halfhearted, hit-and-miss, self-centered prayers that we're accustomed to won't bring revival.

> Prayer is work. It is blessed work, but it *is* work. . . . The chief sin of the church today is laziness. We are lazy about prayer. We're lazy about changing ourselves. We're lazy about good works. We're certainly lazy about praying through for a great spiritual awakening in America.[9]

We must stop leaving the work of prayer to our ministers, our conference leaders, our godly parents, wives, or husbands and get busy with God on our own knees. If we'll take on this work ourselves, we're guaranteed the victory.

> Satan knows better than God's people the power that they can have over him when their strength is in Christ. . . . Satan cannot endure to have his powerful rival appealed to, for he fears and trembles before His strength and majesty. *At the sound of fervent prayer, Satan's whole host trembles.*[10]

Revival must be combined with reformation. Simply put, once God has our attention and we hear His voice, we must obey what He's saying. If we leave obedience out of this discussion, any hope of experiencing a real revival is lost. Seeking God's face of necessity requires us to "turn from our wicked ways." More about this in the next chapter.

Revival must be maintained with prayer. Why did the revivals mentioned earlier all eventually give way to periods of moral and spiritual decline? Though I'm sure there are many identifiable causes, I wonder if people simply stopped praying.

Throughout the revivals the Western world has experienced, after several years, people begin to take the revival for granted. The way this happens is that they forget about the very thing that birthed the revival, prayer. Once continuous and fervent prayer is forgotten, the impetus of the revival is lost and all that is left is the momentum of the past.[11]

Has this happened to Seventh-day Adventists? Do we spend most of our time looking back or looking forward? Are we moving forward under the deliberate power of the Holy Spirit, or are we coasting on the momentum of a past visitation and soon to come to a halt?

Revival must be maintained with prayer.

Revival requires extraordinary prayer. In his closing remarks at the 1976 National Prayer Congress in Dallas, Texas, Dr. J. Edwin Orr strongly stated that Christians could spark a great revival if they "promote explicit agreement and visible union of all God's people in extraordinary prayer."

The word *extraordinary* implies something unusual—something beyond the norm. Maybe it's time for some extraordinary prayer.

On a personal level, maybe this means skipping the noon meal once a week so you can use the lunch hour to get together with others who want to pray. It may mean setting the alarm a half-hour earlier so you can spend the first moments of your day with God. You may want to join the Adventist global prayer network and covenant to pray for the gift of the Holy Spirit at 6:15 each morning.

Corporately, our conference leaders and pastors should be spending more time planning how the churches in a city, district, conference, or union can "promote explicit agreement and visible union in extraordinary prayer."

What about joint prayer meetings of churches within a certain mile radius? How about allotting some time during camp meeting to pray for revival? What if in preparation for a camp meeting, a convocation, or an evangelistic thrust, a week of prayer and fasting was promoted in the churches to prepare the hearts of all present— Adventists and non-Adventists—to receive Christ anew?

We need opportunities for the body to come together in "explicit agreement." Remember Quincy Jones and the "We Are the World" project I mentioned in a previous chapter? When egos and agendas are set aside in pursuit of a common goal, there's no limit to what can happen. And when Christians do this, *watch out!* The book of Acts records the results of "explicit agreement" among believers in prayer—Pentecost!

But one more thing is needed: "visible union." We don't need another excuse to divide and separate. Instead of using our energies in these last days to petition, picket, and push for conferences divided along racial lines, we should use those energies, instead, to arrange large prayer and praise gatherings for people of all ethnic backgrounds, where God's people can seek His face in the "visible union" of Christian brotherhood.

Face it. If we can't get along down here, we won't get the chance to get along up there.

> If anyone says, "I love God," yet hates his brother, he is a liar. For anyone who does not love his brother, whom he has seen, cannot love God, whom he has not seen. And he [God] has given us this command: Whoever loves God must also love his brother (1 John 4:20, 21).

Can we do this? If we can't or won't, we should immediately drop the charade and quit pretending to be Christ's, because we aren't. And we should abandon all hope for revival, because it won't come.

Agreement. Unity. Love. When we seek God's face, we find all three. And if we will give each other a chance, we will find them in the faces and lives of our Christian brothers and sisters, regardless of color, speech, or grade of hair.

Imagine a stadium filled with people of all races and tongues worshiping together and seeking God for revival! What a testimony to the power and grace of God.

Impossible, you say? It's already happening in a group called Promise Keepers—a Christian men's movement that has the look and feel of another Great Awakening. One of the credos of this new movement is the commitment to reach beyond any racial barriers to demonstrate the power of biblical unity. The organizers are determined not to make theirs a "White man's" movement. The results of their efforts are dramatic and awe inspiring.

If revival is to come among us, we must vigorously pursue "visible union." And perhaps we would do well to adopt the vision Coach Bill McCartney—Promise Keepers' founder—has for prayer in this area.

> May every church plead in unison for God's heart and God's solution to bring reconciliation. May our prayer warriors work overtime. Let the pulse of the Body of Christ quicken and not rest until we see change. And let it begin with you and me.[12]

Desperate times call for divinely appointed measures. Prayer— *extraordinary* prayer that is engaged in with the explicit agreement and visible union of God's people—will bring revival.

Revival is God's work. Finally, we must remember that God is the One who sends revival. Matthew Henry said, "When God intends great mercy for His people it is He, first of all, who sets them a praying."

If revival comes, it will be because God moves on the hearts of His children to seek Him with all their hearts. Can you feel Him tugging on your heartstrings right now?

He is ready to supply every soul according to the capacity to receive. Then let us not be satisfied with only a little of this blessing, only that amount which will keep us from the slumber of death, but let us diligently seek for the abundance of the grace of God. . . .

Only to those who wait humbly upon God, who watch for His guidance and grace, is the Spirit given. *The power of God awaits their demand and reception.*[13]

And when that power flows through the church like water over dry ground, thirsty, hurting people will come to us and, like the hummingbird, find refreshment in our Spirit-ripened fruit.

Lord, send revival!

---

1. Ellen G. White, *My Life Today* (Hagerstown, Md.: Review and Herald Publishing Association, 1952), 57.

2. Clifford Goldstein, *The Remnant* (Boise, Idaho: Pacific Press Publishing Association, 1994), 103.

3. *Selected Messages*, 1:121.

4. *What God Does When Men Pray*, 23.

5. *Selected Messages*, 1:121.

6. Ibid., 122.

7. Andrew Murray, *Revival* (Minneapolis, Minn.: Bethany House Publishers, 1990), 20, 21.

8. Ellen G. White, *The Great Controversy* (Boise, Idaho: Pacific Press Publishing Association, 1950), 518, 519, italics mine.

9. Wellington Boone, "Why Men Must Pray," in *Seven Promises of a Promise Keeper*, ed. Al Janssen (Colorado Springs, Colo.: Focus on the Family Publishing, 1994), 30.

10. *Testimonies for the Church*, 1:341, 346, italics mine.

11. *Prayer: Key to Revival*, 19, 20.

12. Bill McCartney, "A Call to Unity," in *Seven Promises of a Promise Keeper*, ed. Al Janssen (Colorado Springs, Colo.: Focus on the Family Publishing, 1994), 165.

13. *My Life Today*, 57, italics mine.

Part 7

And turn from their wicked ways

"Rend your heart and not your garments.
Return to the Lord your God."
—Joel 2:13

"Repentance is a change of heart, not an opinion."
—*Eternity*

Real prayer doesn't ignore sin.
It embraces the Saviour.

C H A P T E R
15

There Is a Saviour

I'd really rather skip this chapter. I'm eager to get to "the good part"—the part about God hearing from heaven and healing our land. Maybe it's just human nature to avoid what is difficult and unpleasant.

But if we shortcut this part of the journey, I'm afraid we'll fail to arrive at our destination. If God had thought it unimportant or unworthy of our notice, He wouldn't have included a call for repentance in His formula for revival. But He did. Why? Because sin is serious business. So serious it cost the Son of God His life. It mustn't be glossed over, played with, ignored, or cherished.

God is calling on His people everywhere to humble themselves, pray, seek His face, and *turn from their wicked ways*. I say it humbly yet emphatically, *if we choose not to let Jesus deal with the sin in our lives, all other attempts to seek Him will be in vain.* Our humility will be a mockery, our prayers will not be heard (see Psalm 66:18), and we will have no desire to seek Him.

Getting serious about sin

I carry in my Bible a copy of Ellen White's outstanding article on revival and reformation entitled "The Church's Great Need." It was published in the *Review and Herald* of March 22, 1887, and can be found in *Selected Messages,* book 1, pages 121 to 127. I keep it for three reasons. One, it inspires and motivates me to pray for myself and my church to experience revival. Two, it shakes me from the lukewarm stupor I often allow myself to be lulled into. And three, it clearly shows how the outpouring of the Holy Spirit can be obtained. It's powerful reading, and I would encourage you to read it for yourself.

This article, which begins with those familiar words, "A revival of true godliness among us is the greatest and most urgent of all our needs," contains no less than six entreaties for God's people to "confess and put away their sins." This is part of the preparation work we must engage in before revival can come.

"Our heavenly Father is more willing to give His Holy Spirit to them that ask Him," she starts, "than are earthly parents to give good gifts to their children. But it is our work, by *confession,* humiliation, *repentance,* and earnest prayer, to fulfill the conditions upon which God has promised to grant us His blessing."[1]

Obviously, confession and overcoming are things we need to get serious about.

What ever happened to sin?

Just mentioning the word *sin* today causes many an eyebrow to raise in condescension. We don't talk about it anymore. In these more politically correct and enlightened times, we talk, instead, of "moral failures" and "deviations," of "disease" and "codependent behavior," of "alternative lifestyles."

"It has been said that one of the characteristics of our age, of its life and thought and theology, is the lack of a sense of sin."[2]

Instead of hating sin and abhorring it for what it has done to the human race and for what it cost the Son of God, we've made peace with it, watered it down, and acted as if there's no devil who goes about as a roaring lion, seeking whom he may devour.

Does this seem too backwoods? Like old-fashioned Bible thumping? If it does, it's because we've lost our sense of the heinousness of sin. Certain behaviors and attitudes have been tolerated as if they were a necessity. And, over time, we accept them as normal and hardly notice them.

But before true revival can come to God's church, we must all allow the Holy Spirit to confront sin in our lives. We must lose our self-righteous smugness that says, "I'm OK and you're OK," and humble ourselves before God, confessing our weakness and love of what He hates—sin.

Beyond the checklist

I realize that in any discussion of sin, most Adventists will immediately seize their mental checklists of all the things they're *not* doing. *Not* drinking (sometimes), *not* smoking, *not* eating this or that, *not* wearing this or that. But the externals are often the easy part of Christianity. It's easy to *look* righteous. But what is God going to have to do to separate us from the pride, the self-seeking, the gossip, and the envy that are eating the soul out of Christ's body and damming up the revival showers of blessing we so desperately need?

Please don't misunderstand. I'm not saying that the externals aren't important. They are, because they reflect the choices and affections of those who claim to be God's separated, holy people. But what goes on in the heart is by far more important.

If all our religion is able to do for us is make us highly moral people who are good citizens and kind to animals, it has failed.

The Christian's life is not a modification or improvement of the old, but a transformation of nature. There is a death to self and sin, and a new life altogether. This change can be brought about only by the effectual working of the Holy Spirit.[3]

Adventists too often stop at behavior. We get the behavior in line (master the externals of dress, diet, etc.) but fail to address the deeper cause.

You may have heard the story about the woman who habitually prayed, "Lord, remove the cobwebs of sin from my heart," at prayer meeting. Each week, when it was her turn to pray, she offered up the same petition: "Lord, remove the cobwebs of sin from my heart." Eventually, this began to peeve one of the younger members in the prayer group, and the next time this older women prayed, "Lord, remove the cobwebs of sin from my heart," the youngster immediately added, "And, Lord, please kill that spider!" It's time we let Jesus lay the ax to the root of our problem.

What wicked ways?

Some reading this may be offended that I'm implying there's a problem to begin with. We don't like to see ourselves as we really are. The truth hurts. That's probably why I've never heard anyone recite Revelation 3:14-17 in a meeting at which favorite scriptures are being shared. Yet this is our condition.

Some in the church would call us to corporate repentance for what Adventists did or failed to do in 1888. I say, Why go back that far? There's enough "sharp criticism, sharp judgment, hasty opinion, unloving words, secret contempt of each other, [and] secret condemnation of each other"[4] in the church *today* that needs repenting of right now!

One of the great tragedies occurring in many of our Black communities is the phenomenon known as Black-on-Black crime. A January 10, 1994, *Newsweek* reports the alarming facts. "The FBI cataloged 23,760 murders for 1992. Roughly half of the victims were black; and in cases where the assailant was known, 94 percent of black victims were slain by other blacks."[5]

But what about Adventist-on-Adventist crime? The things we say and the feelings we harbor against those of our own faith who differ from us in concept and strategy would often cause non-Christians to blush. What percentage of former Adventists no longer want anything whatsoever to do with the church because a fellow Adventist— a brother or a sister in Christ—ambushed them in a weak moment, fired a judgment-seeking missile from his or her mouth, and left them for dead? Have we met the enemy and found that he is us?

In a candid, yet painful admission, Ellen White states:

We have far more to fear from within than from without. The hindrances to strength and success are far greater from the church itself than from the world. . . .

Divisions, and even bitter dissensions which would disgrace any worldly community, are common in the churches, because there is so little effort to control wrong feelings, and to repress every word that Satan can take advantage of. . . . A house divided against itself cannot stand. Criminations and recriminations are engendered and multiplied. Satan and his angels are actively at work to secure a harvest from seed thus sown.

Worldlings look on, and jeeringly exclaim, "Behold how these Christians hate one another! If this is religion, we do not want it."[6]

I ask you. When will this bickering, name-calling, and criticism stop? If it doesn't, Satan won't have to bring persecution to stop us. If he just lets us alone, we'll do ourselves in.

Before we see a fulfillment to the promises of God, "I will pour out my Spirit on all people. . . . And everyone who calls on the name of the Lord will be saved" (Joel 2:28-32), we have work to do. We must turn from our wicked dealings with each other, "rend [our] heart[s] and not [our] garments," and "return to the Lord [our] God" (verse 13).

Repentance must begin with leadership

So how will repentance come to the church? Who leads the way? While we must each answer to God for our own sins and for our own willingness or unwillingness to respond to His call, the leaders in God's church must be foremost in pursuing this experience for themselves and for their members.

At the 1973 Annual Council held in Takoma Park, Maryland, Ralph S. Watts brought a devotional message to the assembled pastors and administrators that brought this issue of repentance home with Spirit-led clarity and urgency.

As leaders we must be truly in earnest in searching our own hearts before we can lead others to the experience of repentance. There must be a determination to correct all evil tendencies in our lives and to become distrustful of ourselves.

After presenting the example of Ezra—his own experience of repentance and conversion first, followed by his intercession for the nation before an assembly of Jewish leaders and laypeople—Watts then made the following practical appeal.

What would happen if in the near future a conference committee or a union committee came together, not to look over an agenda, but to spend all day praying for God's people? Brethren, it's that kind of humility and repentance that God is expecting of His people today. I tell you there would come a revival if we were to spend a whole day—leave the agenda, leave off talking about the problems—and just get on our knees and pray for God's people, pray for the constituency in the conference, and then go out into the churches.[7]

As with the vitality of prayer in the congregation, so it is with the impetus toward repentance among the members—the pastor must set the pace. "Let the priests, who minister before the Lord, weep between the temple porch and the altar. Let them say, 'Spare your people, O Lord' " (Joel 2:17).

Seek the Saviour

Next, we as a people are going to have to turn to Christ and seek Him as our Saviour. Andrew Murray writes:

> The reason so many seek in vain so earnestly for the mighty strengthening of the Spirit in the inner man, and the promised manifestation of Christ which comes through the Spirit, is due to this: they do not seek Christ for what He is, first and last—a Savior from sin.[8]

I distinctly recall the Sabbath afternoon when the realization hit me that I had been relating to Jesus more as a spiritual Santa than as a Saviour from sin. As I walked along the Boise Greenbelt with my family, I saw again, as if for the first time, how my greatest need wasn't for money to pay my taxes or for the down payment on a house, but my greatest need was for a clean heart. I felt my need of His forgiveness and received Him as my Saviour once more.

If we don't consider sin a big deal, however, obedience to Christ becomes less of a big deal too. "You do what's right for you, and I'll do what's right for me—and we'll meet on the corners of Zion and Jerusalem Way in heaven and sing a few rounds of 'Amazing

Grace.' " I know we don't actually say things like that, but do our actions and attitudes betray these sentiments? Are we willing to come to terms with those things in our lives that are stunting our Christian growth and short-circuiting our spiritual power?

There is a Saviour who is eagerly waiting, not only for us to feel regret for our sins, but also for us to experience a fundamental change in our thinking that will result in restored purpose and changed perspective. He does not expect us to do it alone. In fact, our "promises and resolutions are like ropes of sand."[9]

It is God's "kindness [that] leads you toward repentance" (Romans 2:4), not your determination to reform. Yes, God requires the surrender of your will, but that's all you can do. And even this action is prompted by the Holy Spirit. "We can no more repent without the Spirit of Christ to awaken the conscience than we can be pardoned without Christ."[10]

What is keeping you from experiencing the full measure of God's life and love in your life? Are you addicted to pornography? Do you lose the battle with the remote control when lascivious scenes of seduction and illicit encounters parade across the TV screen?

Do you bludgeon your fellow members with harsh, judgmental words and take pride in your ability to "defend" the standards of the church?

Are you eating and drinking to your own detriment instead of to the glory of God?

Are you a thorn in the pastor's flesh—a self-appointed committee of one who feels that it is your duty to "straighten him out" so that he begins to see things your way?

Does hidden rage cause you to strike out against your spouse or children? Do you hit your wife or sexually abuse your son or daughter?

No sinful habit is too big for God. I want to declare to you today that He is not dead. He is risen! And His "hand is not shortened, that it cannot save; neither his ear heavy, that it cannot hear" (Isaiah 59:1, KJV). He is the Saviour who "is able to save completely those who come to God through him" (Hebrews 7:25).

But we must come to Him for healing. Nothing can replace this one step in our walk with God. If we come, He will receive us with open arms and give us the gift of repentance so that we come to hate the sin that "so easily entangles" and turn from our wicked ways.

Come to Jesus now—no, run to Him. If you will humble yourself before Him, confess your sin, and ask for His gift of repentance, will He not give it? Let nothing hinder you. Not your own doubts about your sincerity or Satan's accusations that yours is a hopeless case.

When Satan comes to tell you that you are a great sinner, look up to your Redeemer and talk of His merits. That which will help you is to look to His light. Acknowledge your sin, but tell the enemy that "Christ Jesus came into the world to save sinners" and that you may be saved by His matchless love.[11]

The call to repentance is the final door we must pass through on the road to revival. If our prayers leave it out, we will surely miss the blessing He wants so badly to bestow. Let's not keep Him waiting any longer.

Jesus, I'm an open book,
won't you read every page of my heart?
Jesus, won't you take a look?
Help me find a brand new start.[12]

---

1. *Selected Messages,* 1:121.

2. *Revival,* 87.

3. *The Desire of Ages,* 172.

4. *Absolute Surrender,* 28.

5. Ellis Cose, "Breaking the 'Code of Silence,' " *Newsweek,* 10 January 1994, 23.

6. *Selected Messages,* 1:122, 123.

7. Ralph S. Watts, "The Place of Repentance in Revival," in *Revival and Reformation,* ed. Don Mansell (Hagerstown, Md.: Review and Herald Publishing Association, 1974), 28, 30.

8. *Revival,* 101.

9. Ellen G. White, *Steps to Christ* (Hagerstown, Md.: Review and Herald Publishing Association), 47.

10. Ibid., 26.

11. Ibid., 36.

12. "Jesus, I'm an Open Book," words and music by Dallas Holm, copyright © 1976 Dimension Music/SESAC/Going Holm Music/SESAC. All Rights Reserved. Used by Permission of Benson Music Group, Inc.

Part 8

Then

*"Then will I hear from heaven and will forgive
their sin and will heal their land."*
—2 Chronicles 7:14b

"Satan can no more hinder a shower of blessing from
descending upon God's people than he can close the windows
of heaven that rain cannot come upon the earth."
—Ellen G. White

Real prayer will bring the latter rain.

C H A P T E R

16

Then

The walk back to Jerusalem from Olivet was more a dance than a stroll. Perspiration pasted their clothing to their sun-darkened skin as they ran, but nothing could dampen their spirits today.

Curious onlookers pointed and whispered. Shock? Disappointment? Fear? Yes. These were the emotions they expected to see on the faces of this group. Not joy. Not the giddy exuberance of a child with a new toy. Not ecstacy.

Yet see them as they almost float over the ground. Hear their "Hosannas" and their "Praise the Lords." Were these the same men who had only days before scattered like cockroaches before a bright light when Jesus had been arrested in Gethsemane? Were not these men the same ones who had cowered behind locked doors for "fear of the Jews" after the Miracle Worker's execution?

No. These were not the same men at all.

Those men had died along with their Master. Good riddance.

These bore the same names and faces as the others—Matthew, Andrew, Philip, Thomas, John, etc. But there was something different about them. What was that look on their faces? Ah yes. Many had seen that look before. It was unmistakable.

Jesus. They looked like Jesus.

"John!" Peter nearly trips, trying to walk backward after elbowing his way through to the front of the vibrating knot of disciples now nearing Jerusalem.

"Did you see Him? Did you see the way He looked at us from the cloud?"

"Of course, I saw Him," John replies, trying to slow his pace to keep from trampling his excited friend.

"I've got to tell somebody, or I'll bust," Nathaniel pipes in. "I've never before loved someone so much!"

"Same here," John says, reaching out a hand and turning Peter around by the cloak so that he's facing forward again. "But we must first do what the Master said and wait for the promised blessing."

"I wonder what surprise Jesus has in store for us in Jerusalem?" Matthew ventures.

"Whatever it is, I can hardly wait!" Peter replies.

The days after the ascension were filled with praise and blessing. The disciples were "continually in the temple, praising and blessing God" (Luke 24:53, KJV).

With the money-changers gone, the courts of God's house had returned to normalcy. Worshipers routinely filed in and out without a great deal of bustle or chatter. Ever since the followers of the Nazarene returned to public worship, however, shouts of thanksgiving and praise had reverberated throughout the temple and echoed off the courtyard walls.

What were these people so happy about?

Didn't they realize their "Messiah" was dead? They should have been beating their breasts and mourning instead of rejoicing.

The people just didn't understand. Too bad. But they would. Soon.

The upper room. How it had changed in a few short weeks! Was it only since the last full moon that they had felt such a foreboding sense of gloom and sorrow in that room?

Everyone had felt it. Something was wrong with the Master. The shadows that danced along the floor mimicking the flames from the fireplace seemed longer than usual. The night outside felt clammy and cold. Each bite of food seemed to require twice the usual effort to chew, and swallowing was a chore.

Shame suddenly interrupts their reminiscing. Their conversation that night must have hurt Jesus so! Arguing over who was the greatest—while God Himself stooped to wash their filthy feet!

The words come forth in broken, sob-choked fragments. It is Peter who speaks.

"John—I—I'm—so sorry. I—was—so—so—jealous of—you." The apostle's head is bowed so that his wiry beard, now catching the tears that tumble freely over his cheeks, presses against his bosom.

John puts an arm around the heaving shoulders of his friend and makes a similar confession.

"You were jealous of me, and I burned with envy against you, my friend." Peter turns his head sharply and locks eyes with the one who was always closest to Jesus.

"You? Envious of me? Whatever for? You were closest to Him. What did I that you didn't more?"

"You walked on water, Peter. I was dying to go to Jesus that night. But it was you He called."

"That's only because I asked," the crusty fisherman replies, tears still brimming in eyes that have seen too little sleep lately.

"Will you forgive me?" John says, giving a slight tug on Peter's shoulder.

"I'm ashamed you have to ask. Of course, I forgive you. Will you please forgive my jealousy of you?"

The two men embrace, soon joined by the others, who also utter words of confession and forgiveness.

The room was alive with the mingled sounds of weeping and laughter. They remembered Jesus' prayer that they would be one as He and the Father were one. Now they understood. They went to their knees and talked to Jesus as to a friend. They did not put on airs or try to impress with the flowery phrases of the Pharisees. They simply claimed His promises and asked for the courage and power to share His story with neighbors and countrymen.

With the memory of His parting look at them before the angelic glory obstructed their view, the disciples boldly petitioned for the promised blessing that would fit them for their awesome task. "Jesus is at the right hand of the Father," they reasoned. "He hears us and loves us. The promise will come."

All desire for supremacy vanished. The upper room—formerly a scene of sorrow and place of hiding, but now a chapel of prayer—was mute witness to a new birth. Christ's body was being formed.

For ten days after Jesus left them, the disciples confessed their faults and their previous unbelief. They humbled themselves before their King in heaven and sought His face in continuous, fervent prayer. A spirit of repentance brought great brokenness and great relief.

Passersby heard a symphony of sound coming from the upper-room windows. Songs of praise, words of Scripture, prayers, confession, laughter, and silence daily rained down on a Jerusalem street from this gathering of believers—now numbering 120.

Who knows how it began. Perhaps as a whisper. As gentle as a child's breath when blowing white dandelion fluff. A curtain stirs.

The air suddenly smells sweet. Is it He? Did Jesus come back for a visit? Will He suddenly appear among them as He did that night they were huddled in fear for their lives?

Somewhere, in the distance, a dog is barking. Children are playing on the street below, but their voices are suddenly covered by a deep, thunderlike rumble.

Lights, colors, sound bigger than the shriek of a Galilean storm suddenly fill the room. Heaven itself seems to have descended upon the praying company. Unspeakable joy wells up in the throats of these followers of Christ. The Comforter has come. Peter nudges Thomas and points to a spot just above his head. Thomas nods vigorously without saying a word. Cloven tongues of orange and magenta fire appear over their heads, and as the Holy Spirit fills them, the joy held captive in their throats bursts forth into languages with which they had heretofore been unacquainted.

Pentecost! The inauguration in heaven was complete, and the hearts of Jesus' followers were empty of everything except love for their Master and love for their fellow human beings. The times of refreshing had come. "The sword of the Spirit, newly edged with power and bathed in the lightnings of heaven, cut its way through unbelief. Thousands were converted in a day."[1]

It will happen again.

Instead of the upper room, it will be a living room. A kitchen. An office. A sanctuary. The locations will vary, but the result will be the same.

The great work of the gospel is not to close with less manifestation of the power of God than marked its opening. The prophecies which were fulfilled in the outpouring of the former rain at the opening of the gospel are again to be fulfilled in the latter rain at its close. . . .

Servants of God, with their faces lighted up and shining with holy consecration, will hasten from place to place to proclaim the message from heaven. By thousands of voices, all over the earth, the warning will be given. Miracles will be wrought, the sick will be healed, and signs and wonders will follow the believers.[2]

But this blessing will not come to make us love each other or to motivate us to reach out in love to our neighbors or fellow church members. It does not come to make us obedient or to make us more prayerful. All these things must be done *before* the promised blessing is given. The latter-rain outpouring only ripens the fruit already present on the tree; it does not produce fruit where there is none.

So how are we to obtain the fruit? How can the experience of revival be ours? What can transform our current lifeless worship into the scenes of fellowship and faith that occurred in the upper room with the disciples?

You know the answer. We've examined it, piece by piece, throughout the course of this book.

"If my people, who are called by my name, will humble themselves and pray and seek my face and turn from their wicked ways . . . *then!*"

The promise is certain. It is God who speaks. No loopholes. No second guessing. No disappointment.

Then!

It's emphatic. Unequivocal. Guaranteed.

"*Then* will I hear from heaven and will forgive their sin and will heal their land" (2 Chronicles 7:14).

Then

We need Jesus to hear our cries. Our cries for the Bread of Heaven in a time of famine. "Not a famine of food or a thirst for water, but a famine of hearing the words of the Lord" (Amos 8:11).

Our cries for our children who turn a deaf ear to the Spirit's call. Our cries for a sense of meaning and purpose to return to our worship and to our church.

Our world needs Jesus to hear the cries of the Hutu child who lies beside the body of his mother, eyes without enough moisture to form tears, throat too weak to utter a groan.

Our world needs Jesus to hear the bombs exploding over Bosnia, the shrieks of drowning boat people, the sound of gunfire on a playground, the breaking of a wife's jaw at the hand of a drunken husband.

Does He hear? Oh yes. He's just waiting for His church to hear the same thing.

Do we need forgiveness? Oh yes. He's just waiting for His church to recognize its need.

Do we need healing, physically and spiritually? Oh yes. He's just waiting for His hurting church to fill its prescription for "gold refined in the fire, so you can become rich; and white clothes to wear, so you can cover your shameful nakedness; and salve to put on your eyes, so you can see" (Revelation 3:18).

And it will all come in answer to prayer!

IF we will pray, THEN He will heal our land. The promise is certain. Only one proviso—one contingency. We must pray.

> There is nothing that Satan fears so much as that the people of God shall clear the way by removing every hindrance, so that the Lord can pour out His Spirit upon a languishing church and an impenitent congregation.[3]

So,

Plead as earnestly, as eagerly, as you would for your mortal life, were it at stake. Remain before God until unutterable longings are begotten within you for salvation, and the sweet evidence is obtained of pardoned sin.[4]

We've come to the end of our text and the end of our journey. I hope that you've realized anew the fantastic privileges that are yours as a child of God. I pray that you have gained a clearer understanding about your purpose for being a Christian and have caught a fresh vision for what it means to be a co-laborer with Christ in the building of His kingdom.

I hope God has grown to enormous proportions in your eyes so that you discard the "box" we've all kept Him in and begin to live in the light of this all-powerful Friend. I hope you have heard Him whisper your name and call you "Mine." And as you respond to His call to repentance, I pray that you will turn to find and embrace the love of your life—Jesus.

This book has come to an end, but there's still another chapter to write. Yours. And what you do once you've closed the covers of this book determines what is written in that chapter.

If you close these covers, return the book to the shelf, and resume life as usual, then this really is the end. Thanks for coming along with me on this journey into prayer. Let's pray for each other for strength to endure to the end and for the will to respond to His voice.

If, on the other hand, you hear God calling you by name and you choose to humble yourself and pray, *THEN!* Heaven is the limit.

Reach out your hands and your life for all that He longs to give. It's already yours. All that's needed is for you to take possession. And this you may do *IF . . . you pray!*

---

1. *The Acts of the Apostles*, 38.

Then

2. *The Great Controversy*, 611, 612.

3. *Selected Messages*, 1:124.

4. *Testimonies for the Church*, 1:163.

Tour the wonders of prayer

Do you ever feel like you don't know what to say when you begin your day with God? Or like something is missing from your prayers?

In *Prayer Country*, author Dorothy Watts helps readers experience a refreshing new place, where words flow easily and the prayer life blossoms. Numerous practical exercises will guide you to a place of profound peace, joy, and fulfillment in your communion with God.

US$8.95/Cdn$13.00. Paper.

To order, call toll free 1-800-765-6955, or visit your local ABC.

Conquering the Dragon Within

by Marvin Moore

As the end draws near, Satan—the dragon—attacks Christians with overpowering temptations and enslaving addictions and taunts us with our failures. Can we defeat him?

Marvin Moore, author of *The Crisis of the End Time*, and editor

of *Signs of the Times*, uses the counsel of Scripture, Spirit of Prophecy, and the Twelve-Step recovery program to show that through Christ, character change and victory over sin are certain. This intensely practical book provides hands-on devotional exercises for biblical reflection and study at the end of each chapter. Must reading for those wanting God's assurance and victory in the end times.

Hardcover.

US$13.95/Cdn$20.25.

Available at your local ABC or call toll free 1-800-765-6955.

Books You Just Can't Put Down
from PACIFIC PRESS